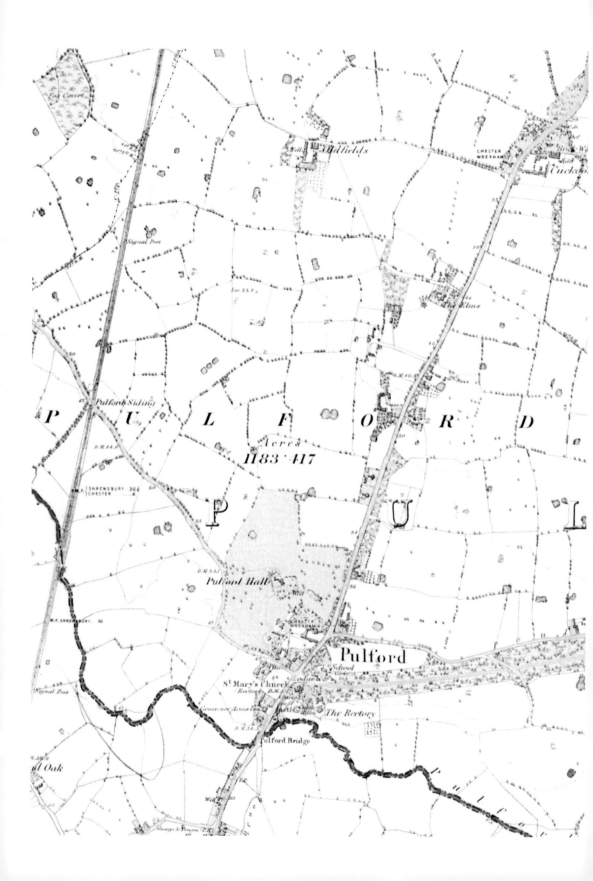

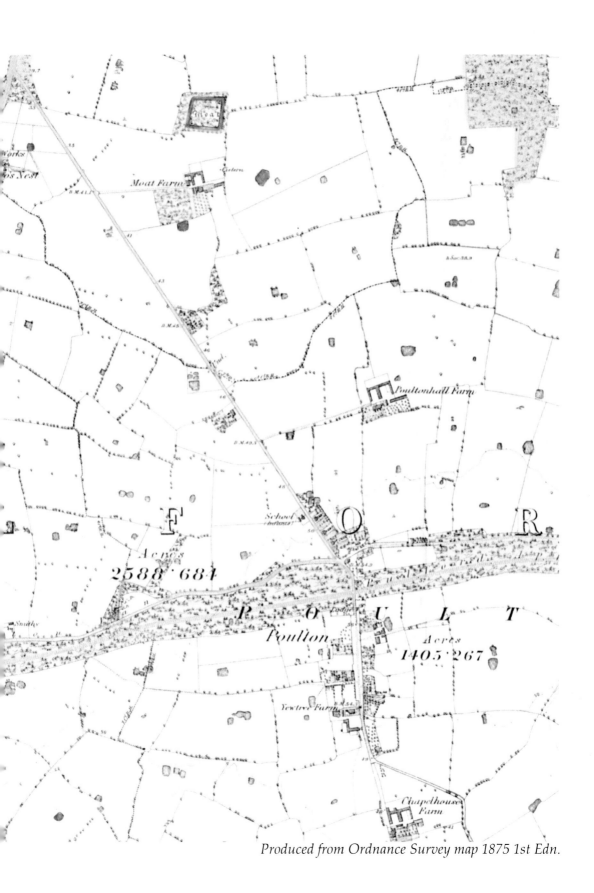

Produced from Ordnance Survey map 1875 1st Edn.

Cover Illustrations (clockwise from top left)

The Grosvenor Arms 1932
Pulford Church 2002
Milking hands at Green Farm c. 1910
Woodhenge (recreated) at the Poulton Archaeological Dig

Through the Ages

Writings on the history of
Pulford & Poulton
in
Cheshire

Pulford & Poulton
Local History Group

Published 2010 by arima publishing
www.arimapublishing.com

ISBN 978-1-84549-454-4
© Pulford & Poulton Local History Group 2010

Printed and bound in the United Kingdom

arima publishing
ASK House, Northgate Avenue
Bury St Edmunds, Suffolk IP32 6BB
t: (+44) 01284 700321

Contents

Foreword

The Duke of Westminster KG CB OBE CD TD DL

Raufe Grosvenor married Joan of Eaton in the 1440s and so started my ancestral connection with Poulton and Pulford. These villages were at that time part of the Eaton Estate, and continued to be until 1919.

In 1541, Henry VIII confirmed Richard Grosvenor in his office of Seneschal (steward of the medieval Great House) of 'Pulton'. In the late 19th century, the 1st Duke of Westminster funded the building of a new church in Pulford. This was designed by John Douglas, an architect responsible for much of the Eaton Estate.

These are two snippets from family archives brimming with documents, maps, charters and deeds, many of which have been used to write this book.

Congratulations to the editing team and to Pulford & Poulton Local History Group for their research. I am delighted to see this book record the fascinating history of the area and for capturing the wealth of local knowledge over the centuries in such a neatly illustrated way.

Introduction

Pulford and Poulton, neighbouring rural communities in the south-west corner of Cheshire, lie on the border with north-east Wales, some five miles to the south of the Roman city of Chester, an International Heritage City. The combined population of Pulford and Poulton is just in excess of four hundred.

The Pulford & Poulton Local History Group was formed in 2000, as a millennium project, at the instigation of the Pulford Village Hall Management Committee. The help and support of Chester History & Heritage (CHH) enabled the Group to start from a good foundation. Its objectives are to carry out research into the history of Pulford and Poulton, to communicate discoveries to a wider audience and promote talks and visits of local historical interest for the educational and cultural benefit of the community as a whole. From its inception, the Group has endeavoured to build an archive of local historical records, documents and photographs that has provided the inspiration for the production of this book. Our History Group is a member of the Cheshire Local History Association and is a contributor to the Association's website.

Members of our Group formed the editorial team, each contributing the results of their individual studies and research. It is from this background that 'Pulford & Poulton through the Ages' has come into being. As such the book cannot be considered a comprehensive record of our history, but more a collection of articles giving a general and varied picture of our past, leading up to the present. Team members have shown their skill, enthusiasm and sheer hard work in creating these writings in just twelve months.

The Archaeological Dig at Poulton under the direction of archaeologist, Mike Emery, has provided a valuable source of information into our early history and continues to unearth new discoveries. This provides the introductory chapter to this book, setting the scene for a variety of writings on many different aspects of life in and around Pulford and Poulton, including architectural history, village enterprise, the life of the church and the Burganey family.

The Grosvenor family, who owned much of Pulford & Poulton into the early 20th century, have left a legacy of many fine buildings throughout the area designed by John Douglas. Architectural features of these buildings are described and illustrated in the 'John Douglas' chapter.

Pulford and Poulton, like so many communities across Britain, not only made a significant sacrifice in the two World Wars, but also witnessed military conflict from Anglo-Saxon times, having a Motte & Bailey castle to help defend Chester against the warring Welsh. This is recounted in the chapter on Military History.

Cuckoo's Nest has a fascinating past. This chapter describes the hive of industrial activity there in its heyday and how it has been transformed recently into a tranquil residential area and select business park.

An agricultural area, Pulford and Poulton have a long history of milk and cheese production and have seen significant changes over the past sixty years. This is explained in the chapter on farming.

Margaret Fair,
Chairman, Pulford & Poulton Local History Group.

Our History Group's website:
www.cheshirehistory.org.uk/pplhg.html

Poulton-Pulford - 7500BC to 1650AD

By Mike Emery

The prehistory of Poulton-Pulford (as for Cheshire in general) has, until recently, been poorly understood. It used to be assumed that Cheshire had virtually no prehistory, that the clay soils were unsuitable for early agriculture, and its large areas of marsh and dense woodland would have supported only a sparse population. In recent years a reappraisal has taken place, as increasing numbers of finds and a few sites have begun to appear, not least in and around Poulton-Pulford.

Surface finds of all periods from the Upper Palaeolithic onwards have been reported for many years, but very few settlement or other sites have been identified. However, recent archaeological, environmental and documentary research is beginning to shed light on the earliest history of the parish.

The first permanent settlers probably arrived around 11,000 BC, towards the end of the last Ice Age.

As the ice-cap began to retreat and melt, a wetland landscape gradually began to emerge in the marshy river valley of the Dee, providing an open landscape of exposed tundra, a marshy surface overlying permafrost, with stunted trees such as Dwarf Birch. Pine and Juniper would follow, later supplemented by Hazel and Elm. Along with the hilltops and slopes of the Mid-Cheshire Ridge, these locations offered the Mesolithic hunter-gatherers (mobile bands) access to a great diversity of plants and animals.

During the earlier part of this period (c.8,000 to 6,000 BC) elk and aurochs were the dominant food animals, but as their habitats decreased in size (as deciduous woodland established itself) so wild pig replaced them. Red and Roe Deer remained important throughout. In addition, beaver, fox, marten, wildcat and bear were hunted mainly for their fur, while water-fowl and fish were hunted for food.

The Poulton-Pulford area would have been a particularly rich area, given that it overlooked a great expanse of water (which would later give its name to both townships--- the 'tun' or settlement by the great pool and the 'ford' or crossing over the pool).

Bows and arrows were important technological innovations of this period. Barbs and tips made from microliths have been found in the parish, from sites overlooking the Old Pulford Brook. For fishing, a variety of barbs and harpoons were made from bone and antler. A simple logboat would have been used in the marshy environs of the parish.

The later Mesolithic (c.6,000 to 4,500 BC) was a period of increasing rainfall in the area. Rising sea levels also led to higher flood-plain levels along the Dee. At this time the transitional forest types of pine, birch, hazel and elm gave way to the mixed oak forest characteristic of the Neolithic (c.4,500 to 2,300 BC).

The new evidence from Pulford-Poulton is adding to the picture of later Mesolithic settlement in the region. Collections of similar material have been found at Aldford, Carden and the Bache Pool. These sites, along with Poulton, are rare examples of lowland activity in the Mesolithic, demonstrating the use of the site during early prehistory. Poulton-Pulford was probably a base-camp from which small communities exploited the surrounding landscape on a seasonal basis. Although the flint collection from the Poulton-Pulford area is relatively small it does provide the starting point for near-continuous activity and occupation over thousands of years.

 The first farming and gradual settlement within the area probably occurred sometime between 4,900 to 4,500 BC. However, the changes that the first farmers brought to the landscape did not happen overnight. The late-Mesolithic population began to create small woodland clearances within which they planted cereals, but hunting and gathering would still have accounted for a significant proportion of the local communities' food. This is borne out by the discovery, during archaeological excavations at Poulton, of several crude plough marks cut into the dense boulder clay that underlay an early Neolithic structure.

Settlement and Monument sites, in Cheshire, are few and far between. Those that have been firmly identified are generally confined to the eastern edge of the county. In the west, apart from Poulton, only one potential site at Churton has been located (though not excavated) through aerial photography.

In general, evidence for Neolithic activity has been confined to scatters of flint tools. Cheshire does not have a readily available source of flint. Instead, early communities exploited the pebbles of lower quality chert (a quartz-based stone resembling flint), found in the local boulder clay and river gravels.

Flints from Poulton-Pulford (photo : A.Wilmshurst)

A stone axe was found near to Brookside Farm (Pulford) but, until recently few other artefacts have been found in the area.

One of the most important questions relating to the area's prehistory, and for Cheshire as a whole, is why Neolithic and later Bronze Age (see below) monuments are so conspicuous by their absence? Is it due to the population being small and scattered? Or could there have been many more monuments, long since destroyed by later ploughing and changing land-use? Does the answer lie in alternative materials being used in an area devoid of suitable stone, materials of a non-durable nature (e.g. wood and leather)? Much of Cheshire, including the Poulton-Pulford area, was probably forested at this time. So, perhaps, Timber Circles and other structures were the dominant form of monument. Such monuments would only show up, in the archaeological record, as post-holes.

The conundrum of the Neolithic is equally applicable to the Bronze Age (c.2,300 to 700 BC). Once again, very little is known about the location of Bronze Age monuments and settlements throughout the region. Those that are known are located towards the eastern borders of the county. And yet, Cheshire lies between two of the greatest concentrations of Bronze Age monuments in Britain, namely the Lake District and North Wales.

Poulton-Pulford lies in the south-western corner of Cheshire on the border with north-east Wales, an area where there is a vast array of known sites covering habitation, farming and burial, many of which have been excavated. Arguably, the most important site lies at Brenig (Denbighshire), barely 30 miles west of Poulton-Pulford. The dense concentration of Bronze Age activity in the Brenig area includes cemetery sites and ring-ditches; recent structures unearthed at Poulton bear more than a passing resemblance to several of the Brenig structures.

Research and excavation at Poulton has begun to shed much new and significant light on the Neolithic and Bronze Age in West Cheshire. The discovery of monuments and ring-ditches at Poulton will have a far wider implication for future research, not only in Cheshire but the north-west in general.

The first major structure on the site was a series of large timber (birch) post-holes 12 in number, forming a roughly circular pattern. These surrounded a much larger oak post placed in the centre of the birch circle. No discernible entrance-ways were recorded.

Very few finds were recovered from this structure, but its form suggests a late Neolithic date (c.3,000 BC). The monument was badly damaged, so interpretation as to its function is problematical. It may have served as a central meeting place for the various local communities coming together at certain times of the year for particular rituals, perhaps associated with burials and/or the exchange of goods. Equally, it may have been a small wooden 'henge'. The evidence for what followed in the Bronze Age, however, is much clearer.

'Woodhenge'
(Artist: Shane
O'Callaghan)

The original Neolithic Timber Circle was pulled down and a new, slightly smaller, structure was erected on the same site c.2,000 BC. This consisted of an incomplete circle of eighteen silver-birch posts delineating an area 15m in diameter.

The circle was interrupted by two entrance-ways, one to the north-west, the other to the south-east, each of which was marked by two external flanking posts. The complete structure was surrounded by a bank and ditch.

Within the enclosure were four small pits containing charcoal, hand-made pottery and quantities of cremated human bone. The pits were, in turn, enclosed by a wide ring of large, predominantly blue, river cobbles.

Bronze Age Ring-Ditch/Cemetery (Artist: Shane O'Callaghan)

The Bronze Age Timber Circle c.1500-800 BC. (Artist: Shane O'Callaghan)

The complexity of such a structure suggests a highly formalised intent, concerned with both burial and ritual. Either side of the south-east entrance, excavation of the timber posts revealed a small concentration of finds. Here, the bases of the posts contained deliberately deposited fragments of cremated human bone, charcoal and pottery. The erection of each post was obviously a deliberate ritual act. It is tempting to argue that these posts represent the ancestors and symbolise the transition from life to death.

However, the greatest concentration of finds, overall, were found within the ring-ditch itself, either side of the south-east entrance (other sections of the ditch were completely barren, as was the north-west entrance).

Reconstruction (in situ) of the Timber Circle (photo: A.Wilmshurst)

Several deposits had been carefully deposited at the base of the ditch. These consisted of the cremated bones of a child, pottery, charcoal and ash, burnt stones and animal bone (mainly pig). The latter probably relates to funereal feasting, prior to internment of the human bone fragments. Also, several Red Deer antler tines were recovered; they had been deliberately sawn. One turned out to be a smooth antler tine with a delicately bored hole. This probably hung around the neck as an ornament. Did it belong to the child? Several horse skull fragments were placed within these deposits. All the finds were carefully sealed by a layer of burnt cobbles.

The deposits represent a final abandonment of the site around 900 BC, demonstrating that it had been carefully, and religiously, maintained for over 1,000 years. All the evidence retrieved from the structures and the artefacts point towards some complex form of funerary rite.

Antler Pick,
Pendant
and Pottery
Fragments.
(photo:
A.Wilmshurst)

Immediately to the south and east of this monument lie at least three more ring-ditches. Each appears to differ in form from the first. Two of these are currently undergoing excavation.

Finally, all the monuments were surrounded by a large enclosure ditch, some 100m in diameter.

This enclosure ditch may well represent the boundary of a sacred zone within which Bronze Age people acted out the rituals which symbolised the transition from life to death. These rituals probably originated even further back in time during the Neolithic period.

The 'Poulton Plaque'

(photo: A.Wilmshurst)

The most intriguing of prehistoric artefacts was retrieved from the site of the second ring-ditch. This was a sub-rectangular fragment of limestone with curiously incised lines (cross-hatching) on each of its faces. Engraved plaques have been recovered, but are extremely rare. They range in date from the Late Neolithic (c.3,000 BC) to the Early Bronze Age (c. 2,000 BC).

The etched design is found on rock or boulder art, but the only two comparable artefact examples were found barely 1Km from Stonehenge. Sculpted out of the local chalk they are similar in size and their etched lines are uncannily alike to the Poulton Plaque. The Stonehenge plaques were similarly deliberately buried.

The function and significance of such plaques is unknown. The Poulton Plaque is equally puzzling. Is it connected to some form of abstract ceremonial or funerary activity? Owing to the rarity of any Late Neolithic-Bronze Age activity in south-west Cheshire (and Cheshire generally), there is no regional parallel. However, flints from the Stonehenge area (Salisbury Plain) have been found at Poulton suggesting that a link existed between the two sites, way back in the distant past. Travel to and from the area would have made use of ancient trackways on the high ground and simple log-boats on the marshy lowland.

Poulton is undoubtedly the centre of a major prehistoric ritual landscape, smaller in size to the more famous sites around Stonehenge and Brenig, but equally important in terms of its significance to the ancestral communities of Poulton-Pulford. Furthermore, a handful of Late Neolithic flints were found in the garden of the Old Rectory, Pulford, during the 'Time Team Big Roman Dig' (2004). More recently, the Poulton Research Project has identified another potential burial ground in Lavister, barely 0.5Km from Pulford parish boundary.

The Poulton Roundhouse (photo: A.Wilmshurst).

This suggests that many more such sites once existed within the Poulton-Pulford area.

THE ROMAN PERIOD

The Roman period (AD c.60-400) is relatively well known at the military establishment of 'Deva' at Chester, and the civilian settlement which was associated with it. This contrasts starkly with the almost total lack of knowledge about the countryside. A few rural settlements and Romanised country houses (villas) have been identified, but there must have been many more farms and industrial communities servicing the military and urban populations, than have so far been identified. The land around Chester, which must have formed the prata legionis ('meadows of the legion'), an area exploited by the military for its agricultural and natural resources, is of particular significance, and Poulton-Pulford was undoubtedly occupied throughout the Roman period.

Roof Tile fragment from Poulton, with stamp mark of the XXth Legion.

Information about Roman rural settlement is, at best, scanty. The number of villa sites in the surrounding countryside is remarkably small; the only recognised sites being Eaton-by-Tarporley, Tattenhall and Crewe-by-Farndon.

The presence of considerable quantities of roof-tiles at Poulton, along with window glass, brooches, fine pottery, coins and other artefacts suggests that a major building is lurking on Chapel House Farm, possibly a Roman villa, temple or villa/temple.

Roman Brooches and Cosmetic Items found at Poulton. (photo: A.Wilmshurst)

In 2004, several gardens were investigated in both Pulford and Poulton, as part of Channel 4's 'Time Team's Big Roman Dig'. In the garden of the Old Rectory, Pulford, several Roman potsherds were found. These were made at nearby Holt, the XX Legion's tile and pottery manufacturing base. This mirrored an earlier collection of similar Roman pottery unearthed prior to the development of Castle Hill Road, Pulford. These finds from the two villages suggests that the area was more densely occupied than previously thought. The link between the two is a minor Roman road that runs from the River Dee, on the western edge of Poulton, through the woods that lie parallel to the Pulford Approach, and which then emerges in the vicinity of the junction of Old Lane and Old Wrexham Road. Another possible Roman trackway has been identified, just north of Lyndale Farm. These minor roads may well have a prehistoric origin, linking native farmsteads.

A recent discovery at the Poulton excavations suggests that another Roman building existed in the landscape. Built of timber, its location is potentially of great significance. It not only underlies a later Medieval chapel (see page 24), but is on exactly the same alignment. It is just possible that this timber building is an early Christian structure dating to the Late/sub-Roman period. Is this the reason why a small medieval chapel and graveyard was established in such an outlandish spot?

In July 2010, a potentially major discovery, and unique to rural Cheshire, was unearthed by the archaeological team working at Poulton. Thousands of Roman pottery sherds had already been recovered from the site and their source of origin, for the most part, identified. However, although there are known production centres at urban/industrial settlements, such as Holt in north Wales, Chester, Northwich, Middlewich and Wilderspool in Cheshire, there are certain ceramic wares for which there is no known provenance. It has long been known that there must be other kiln sites within a radius of 5 to 20 miles of the legionary fortress at Chester. The discovery and location of kiln sites can add greatly to our knowledge of trade, technical advances and exploration of local and regional resources throughout the Roman period. Furthermore, they can help to resolve the problem as to who were responsible for the construction of the kilns and the production of the ceramics.

The recent unearthing of 'kiln-furniture' at Poulton, such as 'wasters and spacers' along with dense concentrations of carbonised wood, ash and burnt stone, strongly suggests that a Roman kiln(s) produced pottery on the site. The ongoing excavations of the kiln site at Poulton offer an exciting and hitherto unexpected opportunity to further our understanding of rural and industrial settlement sites in Cheshire. It also emphasises the potentially increasing importance of the parish throughout the Roman period.

Post-Roman and early Saxon settlement in the area is little understood: to a large extent this is because little durable material culture was produced at the time, which has meant that few finds have been made, even in large-scale excavations, such as at Poulton. However, at the end of the Saxon period, the Domesday Book gives us a snapshot of settlement patterns prior to, and during, the Norman Conquest. Both Pulford and Poulton are mentioned in the

Domesday survey, a detailed record of land ownership designed to give a clear picture of the resources available to the feudal overlord of the estate and, ultimately, the king. Essentially, a means by which tax assessments could be made based on the number of fields under cultivation and how many animals and people inhabited the area.

In 1086, the Poulton population probably numbered somewhere between forty & fifty individuals, or ten to twelve households. Pulford was much smaller, the land supporting one or two households.

The manors were owned by an Earl Eadwine. Unusually, for a pre-Conquest landowner, he continued as an under-tenant of Robert Fitz Hugo on most of his holdings around Malpas. This probably means that he did not take part in the rebellion against William I in 1069, which led to severe reprisals by the Normans on the people and land of Cheshire. Little is known about Eadwine. However, despite his English name, he appears to have been a Welshman, and is known in other sources as Eadwine of Tegeingli.

Eadwine's hold on the manor of Poulton did not, however, continue after the Norman Conquest. Instead it is listed as being held by a Richard Pincerna, who also held a second estate at nearby 'Calvintone' (a 'lost' village possibly located between Poulton and Eaton). It was his son or grandson, Robert who donated a part of the manor of Poulton to William, Abbot of Combermere, to found an Abbey here.

So, how and why was an abbey established in Poulton? The Norman Conquest occurred during a time of great ecclesiastical reform, when old religious houses were being reorganised along stricter lines. A renewed interest in endowing monastic institutions led to a flurry of new foundations, especially on rural sites, contrasting with the Saxon preference for foundations in towns or around which towns had grown. The Cistercian order was especially interested in taking deserted sites, which they could mould to their own tastes; some communities copied the layouts of their mother house and took the opportunity to expand when they later prospered.

Cistercian houses were the most numerous in Cheshire: there were four, at Combermere, Poulton, Stanlow and Vale Royal. Combermere was the earliest, dating from 1133, when it was founded as a Savignac house. Following the joining of the order with the Cistercians in 1147, thereafter it became Cistercian itself.

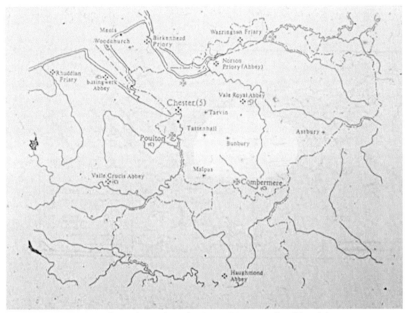

Map of Medieval Religious Houses in Cheshire
(after CW Arch.Service)

The specific foundation date of Poulton Abbey is subject to debate; it was certainly founded sometime between 1147 and 1153, as a daughter house of Combermere (see above map).

The foundation charter of the Abbey of Poulton has survived, as part of the collection of documents preserved by its successor, Dieulacres Abbey, near Leek in Staffordshire (British Library MS Cotton Nero III f.215). The abbey was founded during a period of great national instability, largely a consequence of the devastating civil war between King Stephen and Matilda.

Ranulph II, Earl of Chester and grandfather of Ranulph de Blundeville, had been taking an active part in the civil wars being waged by the two rival claimants to the English throne. The Earl had married Maud, a niece of Matilda, and on account of this relationship, and a personal grudge against Stephen, he took the side of the Empress in the wars. In 1141, he had captured Stephen at Lincoln.

On 29th August 1146, it was the turn of Earl Ranulph II to be captured by King Stephen at Northampton. The Welsh took immediate advantage of the Earl's imprisonment to ravage and lay waste the hinterland of Chester. Robert Pincerna was hereditary 'botelier' or butler, responsible for the Earl of Chester's household. A wealthy landowner, he granted a half-manor of Poulton to the Cistercian monks of Combermere, to found an abbey and pray for the health and safety of the Earl, grandfather of Ranulph de Blundeville. To this end a group of monks left Combermere to establish the Abbey of Poulton in c.1153, under it first abbot, Ralph.

Poulton was founded in the heyday of Cistercian colonisation in England. It is interesting to observe that a great many religious foundations were made during the immense upheaval created by civil war. The great lords, such as the Earl of Chester, endowed monasteries as almost a kind of atonement for the atrocities that they committed during a particularly violent and bloody conflict.

The Cistercians were the great reforming monks of the twelfth century. The order took its name from the first foundation established in 1098 at Citeaux (south of Dijon, France), in an area of dense forest and marshy bog-land, the favoured locations of many succeeding foundations. The monks adhered to the strict ideals of St Benedict, in contrast to what they saw as the laxity rampant in the black-robed Benedictine and Cluniac orders.

They preferred to found their houses in desolate places and to reflect the austerity and poverty of the order, both in the lives of the monks and in their buildings. The houses were intended to be self-sufficient and, unlike other orders, they refused to accept tithes.They were also exempted, by Papal edict, from paying tithes in parishes in which they pastured sheep, a source of later friction in neighbouring Pulford and Dodleston. Furthermore, any contact with lay peasant agriculture was expressly forbidden (it is not surprising that there are numerous records of violent incidents between monks and local villagers, some of which ended in murder).

Despite their austere ideals, the Cistercians quickly became wealthy, especially through their acquisition and development of land. Their holdings became profitable through their skill at transforming the landscape; their activities included reclaiming marshlands and heaths (the Pulford Brook, that flows through both Pulford and Poulton, was created by the Poulton monks to bring marshy areas of the River Dee floodplain into cultivation and pasture).

The Cistercians were predominantly sheep farmers and had a huge impact on the rural landscape. It is worth noting that the ransom of Richard I was paid in wool, which represented a whole year's output from Cistercian abbeys. Their farms were based on the monastic grange, a system initiated by the order. These were worked by the 'conversi', hired labourers who were lay brothers within the monastic community. The Cistercians enhanced the status of agricultural work for monks, but the tasks of clearing forests, draining marshes and overseeing flocks and crops in wild and desolate places were beyond the powers of unaided choir monks; the Cistercians, by recruiting cottars and small freeholders as lay brethren, opened up the religious life to peasant classes previously excluded from it, thereby creating a highly productive labour force. Many, if not all, would have been recruited from Pulford, Poulton, Dodleston and Churton.

Properties acquired through donations, endowments or other means required skilled management; this factor, plus the need to institutionalise the figure of the lay-brother, led to the grange system. Granges were a characteristic feature of the Cistercian economy, organised mainly as independent farms to control the monastic lands and be responsible for their agriculture. In cases such as Poulton, where the Abbey itself was later removed to Dieulacres, the surrounding monastic properties were retained and continued to be worked by the existing granges, albeit under the control of the new abbey. Poulton, however, remained the centre of Dieulacres' agriculture wealth in Cheshire, establishing new granges at Dodleston and Churton (possibly Kinnerton).

The grange itself would have resembled a small village with large storage barns, a smithy, a small chapel, stables, a brew-house, fish-processing sheds and usually a guest house.

Some of our finest ruined abbeys were built by the order--- like Fountains and Rievaulx in Yorkshire, and Valle Crucis at nearby Llangollen. But there were once many more Cistercian houses than the few we can see today. Most of the original sites are now close to invisible, the monastic walls either incorporated into later buildings or quarried away until nothing survives above ground. In some cases, as at Poulton, even the locations of former structures have been lost. However, Poulton is unusually well-documented in Charters and Endowment records. Some of the documents are currently in the Staffordshire Record Office, but many are still retained in the Eaton Archive collection, accessible through the Cheshire Record Office (Chester).

Robert Pincerna's charter stated that the monks were to receive one half of the estate in Poulton which he held of his master, the Earl of Chester. Later, his son (or grandson) granted them the other half of the estate. The rights of protection and custody, which would normally have been retained in the Pincerna family, were now assumed 'de facto' by the Earls of Chester.

Hugh Cyveliok, the fifth of the Norman Earls of Chester, made several gifts of his own, including lands and pastures to the north of the adjacent manor of Dodleston (Gorstella). When Earl Hugh died in 1181 he was succeeded by his son, Ranulph III 'de Blundeville. Ranulph confirmed his father's donations to the monks of Poulton. He also granted them fishing rights in the River Dee at Chester. The Earl and other prominent landowners continued to endow Poulton Abbey with grants of land locally; these included lands in Pulford, Dodleston, Balderton, Gorstella, Aldford and Churton. Such grants further emphasised the monks' gradual consolidation of their influence on the landscape and their creation of a large local land-block that was predominantly Cistercian. In all, it is estimated that by the end of the 14th century, the monks possessed some 3,000 acres, two-thirds of which were pastoral and predominantly given over to sheep farming.

Other grants included houses and gardens in Chester, several of which were located in Pepper Street. In addition they had salt-pits in Middlewich. Further endowments of land were made in Christleton, Harthill, Byley and Eaton-by-Tarporley. Such widespread endowments demonstrate that the Poulton monastic estate was a power within Cheshire for some 300 years, and that Poulton was the Cistercian's richest estate in the county.

The wealth and impact of the Poulton monastic estate can be assessed by the records of the the Mize, a tax collected when Edward, the son of Henry VI, was created Earl of Chester in 1454. Poulton was assessed at £1 7s 6d, a high figure which can be contrasted with the 12s 10d for Pulford and compared with the rich medieval market town of Malpas assessed at £1 12s 0d. In essence, Poulton was rated third behind Malpas and Chester.

Poulton, as an abbey, was unusual in being very short-lived. Medieval documents show that it lasted only until about 1220, when the monastery relocated to Dieulacres (Staffordshire). Poulton was then converted into a grange.

The 'Chronicle of Dieulacres' states that the monks of Poulton had been exposed to the recurring danger of Welsh raiding. That Earl Ranulph de Blundeville, aware of their precarious existence, decided to relocate them to a site at Dieulacres, near Leek in Staffordshire. However, the Chronicle also offers an alternative reason for the move. The story goes that the Earl's divorce from his first wife, Constance of Brittany, and his subsequent marriage to Clementia de Fougeres, underpinned his real motive for translating the monks from Poulton to Dieulacres. That one night he had a dream in which he saw the ghost of his father, Earl Ranulph II, in whose name the abbey of Poulton had been founded. The Earl was instructed by his grandfather to establish a new abbey in the vicinity of Leek, at a place where there had once been a chapel dedicated to the Blessed Virgin Mary, the patron saint of the Cistercian order. The monks of Poulton were to abandon their old abbey and move to the new site. In the dream it was also prophesied that the Pope would place England under Interdict (national excommunication under which all churches would be closed, none could receive the sacraments and thereby all would be living in a state of sin and mortal fear for their souls). Furthermore, that he should go to Poulton Abbey where the monks would hold mass and give him the sacraments, therefore saving him from potential damnation. On awakening from his dream he told his wife who is said to have declared 'Deux encres'; Earl Ranulph declared that the new foundation would be called Dieulacres (God's acres/land).

When Pope Innocent III duly placed England under Interdict in 1208, the Cistercian monks of Poulton, notoriously independent, openly ignored the Pope's edict and allowed the Earl to attend their services and receive the sacraments. In 1220, the last recorded Abbot of Poulton, Richard, led a body of monks to found a new abbey at Dieulacres.

Poulton itself was reduced to the status of a Grange. However, it was still run and overseen by a small number of monks who also maintained and fulfilled religious services at the Chapel of Poulton. It remained the focus of the new abbey's continued agricultural exploitation of this part of Cheshire.

Poulton Chapel overlooking the Old Pulford Brook (Artist : Jane Braine)

Little is known of the history of the Chapel at Poulton. Abbot Richard left Poulton with his monks in c.1220 and the Chapel was first mentioned in a charter of 1250. At first glance this would suggest a continuity between the two establishments. It was once thought that the chapel was founded by the monks to serve the local community after the main monastic community had relocated to Staffordshire. However, recent archaeological work has revealed that the earliest origins of the Chapel predate the foundation of Poulton Abbey; that it has a pre-Conquest (late Anglo-Saxon) origin, possibly as early as the 1020's AD.

Rural chapels were important in medieval Cheshire since few townships were wealthy enough to maintain their own church. The Chapel at Poulton has, to date, yielded 487 burials, some of which pre-date the earliest phase of construction of the Chapel. This proves that the site was used as a graveyard before any building work on the Chapel commenced. The fact that it is situated in a relatively isolated position probably reflects local folk-consciousness and memory of the site being an ancestral home of the dead dating back to prehistoric times.

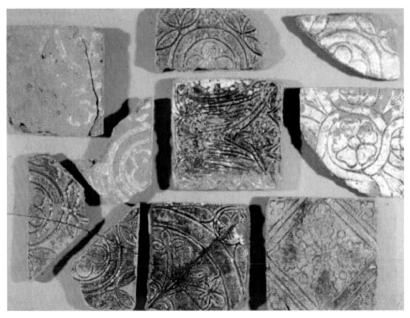

14ᵗʰ/15ᵗʰ century floor tiles from Poulton Chapel

The Chapel underwent several phases of construction. Initially, it was a simple single cell structure built of red sandstone with a rammed clay floor. In time (13th-14th century), the floor was replaced by a mixture of decorated, and undecorated, glazed floor-tiles.

Little is known as to its early history, though the Assize records of Chester occasionally shed light on the odd event. On 14th September 1400, one Ieuan Gogh was indicted for lying in wait near the 'Grange Chapel' with the murderous intent to cause bodily harm on a Thomas Quythod.

Other documents reveal frequent disputes between the 'men of Eaton' and the 'men of Poulton'. In 1414, a Nicolas of Poulton, 'fellow monk of the Abbot of Dieulacres' was bound over in the sum of £100 for violent conduct towards the servants of John de Eaton. Such a large sum indicates the gravity of the offence(s) and bears witness to the increasing friction between the two townships. For a man of God, Nicolas of Poulton was a decidedly unsavoury character!

Sometime in the 15th century the monks of Dieulacres leased out Poulton and its farms to a local Cheshire family, the Manleys. The earliest extant record dates to 1493, when John Manley leases land and buildings from the Abbot of Dieulacres. This lease is confirmed in 1504 by his son, Sir Nicholas Manley. However, the Abbot did not completely sever all ties between Dieulacres and its mother site at Poulton, for the lease included a proviso that '...the said Nicholas Manley will receive and entertain the said Abbot and twelve mounted companions twice a year for six days, and also that he will entertain the cellarer and other servants of the house (Dieulacres) when they shall pass towards Poulton'. (Eaton Charters: Henry VII 22).

For their part the Manleys were excused having to provide wine, fresh salmon and oysters on these occasions!

It was either Sir Nicholas or his father John who was responsible for the major reconstruction of the Chapel. The original single cell building was augmented by the addition of an eastern chancel and a tower to the west. Blue and white tiles were imported from Spain to decorate the floor of the chancel. In essence, the Manleys created a private family chapel.

In 1506 Sir Nicholas leased lands in Poulton to his brother William. It was this brother and his sons who founded Lache Hall. Sir Nicholas died in 1520, but not before leaving his last will and testament; 'I, Nicholas Manley, whole of body and perfect of mind, intending to avoid discord after my death, make my will. My body to be buried in the chapel of Pulton in the chancel there. After my death and my wife's, a priest to be found to sing there for my soul...Residue of the issues to be spent on the Chapell of Pulton... Henry Manley, my son, to have my farme and holding, held of the Abbot of Dieulacres...provided that he dwell in the hall of Pulton wherin I now do dwell, and do not sell without the advice of my executors'. (Earwaker MS. Parcel 16 Wills).

Poulton Chapel Foundations and Manley Burial in the Chancel

In 1997, a burial was discovered within the chancel that has been tentatively identified as that of Sir Nicholas.

It was placed in a central position facing the altar and, unlike most of the burials excavated within and outside the chapel, was complete and undisturbed. He was 6 feet tall and lived to 70 years of age. Medical analysis of his bones shows that he once broke a leg which had healed very well. It proves that he must have had access to the best medical treatment available. Dr Charlotte Roberts, of Bradford University, an expert in biological anthropology, stated that '...an orthopaedic surgeon today would be quite happy at the way it has healed'.

Today, the Poulton Archaeological Research Project has a close partnership with John Moore's University, Liverpool, which has a specialist forensic science department. Students and staff are actively engaged in researching the medical histories of the burials from the Chapel. They are engaged in DNA analysis, dietary habits, pathology and facial reconstructions of the medieval population of Poulton and Pulford. In time the early inhabitants of the parish will be brought to life, to give a visual realisation as to what they looked like, how they lived and worked, what they ate, what medical conditions they suffered from and how they died.

Close-up of burial within the Chancel (from 'Meet the Ancestors' BBC2).

The Abbey of Dieulacres was dissolved on 26th August 1543. The manor and Chapel of Poulton were subsequently granted to Sir George Cotton and his wife Mary. The Cottons sold part of the manor to Thomas Grosvenor. The Manleys continued to reside at Poulton Hall but finally sold their entire estate at Poulton to Richard Grosvenor, in the reign of Elizabeth I (1558-1603).

The family had been in financial difficulties for some time, not least through the unscrupulous actions of a certain

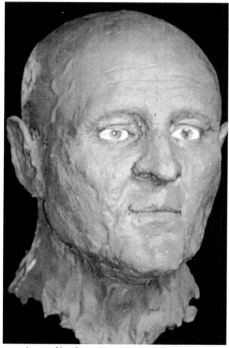

A medical artist, Richard Neave, of Manchester University, is an acclaimed expert in facial reconstruction of skulls. He declared that 'Sir Nicholas was obviously European and was quite a good-looking man' (above).

Henry Brereton. A petition of John Manley (1558) claimed that his family had been deprived of rights to his father's leasehold property, Poulton Grange, by means of a forged will. (Cheshire C.R.O. DDX 18/16)

The Manleys were also caught up in the religious turmoil of the sixteenth century; they were condemned as recusants in Elizabeth I's reign and accused of harbouring Catholic priests. The Visitation of 1592 found that an illegal nocturnal marriage without banns had taken place in the Chapel (Beck 1969, 91).

The last Manley, John, died in 1598 and the entire estate passed into the hands of Richard Grosvenor.

Little is known as to the Chapel's fate during the seventeenth century, direct documentary evidence being scarce.

The last major historical event associated with Poulton Hall and the Chapel was the English Civil War. The central role of Chester is familiar, with its royalist garrison enduring a protracted siege until its capitulation on 3 February 1646. The preceding 3 years saw the billeting of Parliamentary troops in the surrounding villages, including Pulford, Poulton, Farndon, Doddleston and Eccleston.

The Chapel, with its commanding site and its tower was a perfect lookout post, and its masonry structure would probably have been both defensible and habitable.

Sir Peter Leycester described the Chapel as being 'in decay' when he visited Poulton in 1673.

By 1718 the Chapel is recorded as having been completely demolished and that 'nothing at all is now left of it' (Bishop Gastrell).

The Grosvenors continued to hold the manor and all the land in the township of Poulton until early in the twentieth century, when a large part of their estate was sold off. The estate, which included the site of the Chapel, was ultimately acquired by the Fair family and continues in their ownership. It was the discovery of a glazed ceramic floor-tile, on the Chapel site, by Gerry Fair in the 1960s that first hinted at the complex history of Poulton. One small tile that has led to the gradual understanding of some 9,500 years of the parish's history.

The 'Gerry Fair Tile' (photo: A.Wilmshurst).

Acknowledgements.

The Poulton Research Project is sponsored by the Duke of Westminster, the Grosvenor Estate, the Fair Family, Ralph Fiennes, Friends of Poulton, Chester Round Table, Liverpool John Moores University and many others too numerous to mention.

Footnote: The Poulton Archaeological Dig (Poulton Research Project) is independent of the Pulford & Poulton Local History Group and is under the direction of archaeologist, Mike Emery, and the Project's Board of Trustees.

The Eaton Hall Light Railway

By Kate Fairhurst

Miniature Railway, Eaton, Chester

In 1894 the Hon. Cecil Parker, agent to Hugh Lupus, the first Duke of Westminster commissioned Sir Arthur Heywood to design and build a fifteen inch gauge railway connecting Eaton Hall to the Great Western Railway sidings at Balderton. At this time, all household supplies and the many tons of coal needed to heat and light Eaton Hall were carried by carters using horse-drawn vehicles. The railway, which would provide a more effective system of transport, would also have special carriages to bring guests to and from Eaton for the many social events there. In addition it would have a branch line running parallel to the Wrexham road at Belgrave to the brickworks and yard at Cuckoo's Nest. The design allowed for five thousand tons per year to be carried: mainly of coal, timber, road metal and bricks. The total cost was just less than six thousand pounds.

Plan & Section of Eaton Railway

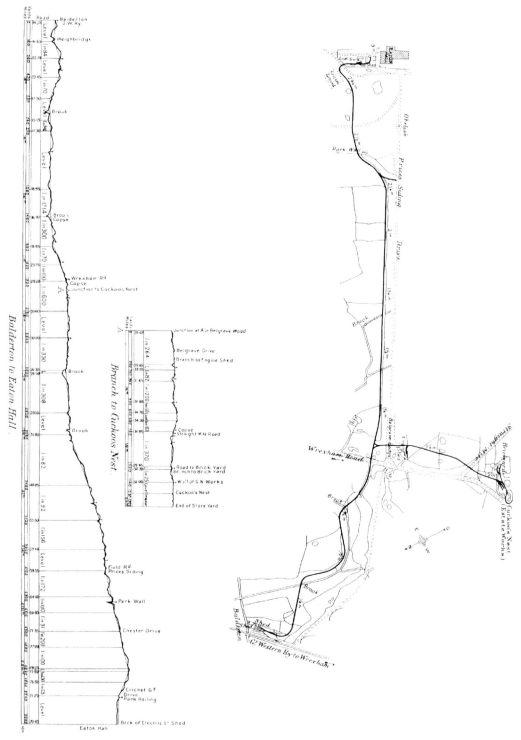

[1] *The route and elevation of the railway, courtesy Plateway Press collection*

The line was built to last, and the steel rails were carried on cast iron sleepers. When work began on the laying of the track in August 1895, Sir Arthur Heywood himself worked for the first fortnight with a beater, rammer and crowbar thus demonstrating to some of his sixteen staff the method of line construction. By Christmas the first three mile section to Eaton Hall had been completed and the rest of the line was finished by May 1896. The total length of the line was four and a half miles. It had to be as unobtrusive as possible and so ran unfenced through the fields, across the Wrexham road and alongside the main drive to Eaton Hall where it terminated. Heywood described its appearance as 'that of a narrow garden walk'. Deep ditches were dug where it crossed between fields to prevent cattle from straying and girder bridges were built over these to carry the track.

²The train crossing a girder bridge, courtesy of the Grosvenor Family Archive

After the line entered Eaton Hall grounds a branch line forked south to pass an engine shed at Belgrave, which is on the site of the present Grosvenor Garden Centre. It continued over the fields, crossing Straight Mile and on to the estate yard and brickworks at Cuckoo's Nest. It was the duty of all employees on the Eaton Estate to ensure that the line was kept clear of any obstacles. The yardmen were responsible for keeping the points in good working order at all times, oiled at least once a week and free from ice in the winter. The smooth running of the operation was the responsibility of the superintendent of the line, a Mr Forster.

[2]Shelagh at the estate yard circa 1910, courtesy of the Grosvenor Family Archive.

Three steam locomotives were used, the first being Katie (see previous page), named after Katherine, Hugh Lupus' wife. A replica of 'Katie' can be seen at Eaton Hall on the days when the gardens are open to the public. The second locomotive was called Shelagh (pictured above), the popular name of the second Duke's wife, and the third was Ursula, named after one of his daughters. Other rolling stock included thirty wagons for carrying coal, bricks and road metal, a sixteen seater bogie passenger car, a parcel van and a brake van. These travelled at an average speed of ten to twelve miles per hour.

Driver Harry Wilde kept a log of the notable passengers and visitors who were brought to Eaton Hall on the train. He noted that in 1905 Winston Churchill travelled in the passenger carriage as did Edward VII later that year, no doubt to attend one of the many shooting parties that were held there. Other well known personalities were Baron Rothschild and the King of Spain. [3]George Ridley, who much later became Chief Agent of all the Eaton Estates, describes how in 1926 'the shoot' had been transported by the Duke's private train to an area south of the hall where the beaters (estate workers dressed in leather- belted white smocks, brown leggings and scarlet hats for visibility), were encircling the 'Brickyard Wood'. No doubt the game they shot was transported back to Balderton sidings in the Eaton railway parcel van and then on to London.

The line entering the works yard from the brickworks in the early 1900s. Courtesy Plateway Press collection

The Heywood steam engines were found to have an inherent design fault in their fireboxes and after Sir Arthur's death in 1916, it became more difficult to obtain spares for repairs. After the First World War a petrol locomotive was acquired and the steam engines were only used for special occasions.

In 1942 it was decided to dismantle 'Katie' and 'Ursula', perhaps as a result of the wartime drive for scrap metal. The line to Eaton Hall continued to be used to transport coal and timber to the hall and to the wood yard at Belgrave, but by 1944 the section to Cuckoo's Nest was no longer in use. The line was discontinued in 1947. At this time Eaton Hall was leased to The War Department, and as the army had its own fleet of vehicles, the little railway was no longer required. Mr Harold Gordon of Poulton recalls that a few of the rails were used to make the cattle grid on the drive to Poulton Hall Farm where he worked.

Pulford WI enjoys an outing on the train circa 1930.

The railway was in operation for over fifty one years. For most of its working life, it had only two engine drivers. The first was Harry Wilde who came to Eaton with Sir Arthur Heywood in 1895 to assist in the construction of the line.

He held the position of engine driver for over thirty seven years. The second was Harry Morgan, a local man, who drove the train until the line closed. Other train workers included two labourers who were responsible for loading and unloading, and two brakemen who rode at the back of the train.

[1]Harry Wilde (seated) with Harry Morgan, courtesy of the Grosvenor Family Archive.

The responsibilities of the railway workers were stipulated in the regulations. There were twenty three rules for the driver. He had to observe carefully the county council regulations (in regard to crossing the public roads), which stated that every train should stop not less than ten yards from the road and the brakeman should proceed to the centre of the road with a red flag (or red lamp after dusk) which should be waved as a warning to oncoming vehicles. No train should cross the road at a speed greater than five miles per hour. Signalling regulations required the driver to give three short whistles when he needed the brakes to be put down and one short whistle when they were to be released. A continuous whistle was a call for assistance and any workman within ear-shot should proceed at once to the spot.

Today very little evidence remains of the railway. An unexplained dip in the kerb diagonally opposite the drive to Eaton Hall marks the place where the line crossed the Wrexham road. The engine shed at Belgrave is now an office at the Grosvenor Garden Centre and can be seen through the metal gates on entering. The carriage shed and coal store buildings remain almost unchanged near Eaton Hall.

[4]The train for Shrewsbury arriving at Balderton station hauled by a GWR 2-6-0 locomotive c. 1929.

⁴The train for Chester approaching Balderton station c.1929.

References:

1. *Minimum Gauge Railways by Sir Arthur Percival Heywood and Sir Arthur Heywood and the Fifteen Inch Gauge Railway by Mark Smithers (Plateway Press).*

2. *F.Wilde Collection Adds 1026/3.*

3. *'Bend'Or Duke of Westminster', by George Ridley.*

4. *Photographer: Geoff Richmond, photos courtesy of Terry Broadhurst.*

The work of John Douglas in the Parish of Pulford & Poulton

By Derek Venables.

The work of Chester architect John Douglas, (1830 – 1911) has been well documented and evidence of his work in the North West of England, (Chester in particular) and in Wales continues to be widely appreciated. The first Duke of Westminster provided John Douglas with an extensive commission for Eaton Estates architectural improvement in the late nineteenth century, and, in and around the villages of Pulford and Poulton, many buildings reveal his distinctive architectural style.

In his work there is a balance and proportionality of classic architectural style, a use of traditional features, and a pursuit of local materials and craftsmanship that recalls the work and theory of William Morris and the Arts and Crafts movement. He reaches out in church design to the neo-Gothic with some evidence of the Germanic influences of the Victorian era (originally apparent in Prince Albert's influence in the design of Balmoral in the 'schloss' featuring) whilst introducing his own individualistic style.

In many public buildings, in the larger houses, and

Spiral chimney.

Channelled herring-bone indent.

in some cottages he often incorporates a cylindrical spiral chimney pattern (known locally as 'barley-sugar style') or as a variation in channelled 'herring-bone' indent on high chimney stacks.

Roofing is usually red tile or Welsh slate with gable ends carrying a Dutch style rounded finish with added pargeted decoration in larger houses or a half-timbered finish to the gable frontage.

In the use of local red sandstone there is often a compatible aslar colour variant, and there is sustained interest in the Ruabon glazed brickwork, the string courses separating storey levels, and in the blue-brick diamond (diaper introduction) decorative patterning to the upper walls. In these upper walls there is sometimes an additional decorative feature of hanging tiles.

Pargeted gable decoration.

Window mouldings, mullion and sill, are individually made in highly crafted brickwork to reveal particular skills, while window-panes contain intricate leaded-light diamond-shape work. Main doors and porches have specific Douglas characteristics, as they reveal impressive attention given to stone and/or brick surrounds, substantial pillar woodwork, and suitable wrought-iron hinge, and stud work.

Moulded brick string coursing.

The intention in this article is to examine and describe a representative sample of the work of John Douglas in the exterior design of buildings in Pulford and Poulton as itemised and considered in 'The Work of John Douglas' by Edward Hubbard published in 1991 by The Victorian Society. In that excellent work the author provides extensive reference to Eaton Estate Office records and papers which are always of particular interest. Since 1991 traditional dairy farming locally has continued to follow the national decline. Farmers have retired and farm -houses have often been separated from farm buildings. When modernised and improved within, such buildings become attractive to those seeking the peace and tranquillity of rural life. Fortunately the distinctive John Douglas design to the

The parish church of St. Mary, Pulford.

building exterior has been largely retained and in some cases new building has incorporated reference to his design style so helping to preserve architectural unity.

The Parish church of St. Mary, Pulford (1884) is a typically well-proportioned building having, in the Germanic style, a wood-shingled spire (octagonal in shape) with miniature hip dormers and four pinnacles. The spire was restored to the original John Douglas design after the disastrous fire on Wednesday 31st. July 1991 although the oak shingles were replaced with red cedar shingles.

Spire

The main walled structure of the church is of local red sandstone with side windows to the nave being of simple form with some tracery below plain heads.

The east and west windows, however, are much more intricate having a four mullion head interlacing around a geometrical stone rose motif.

Church of St. Mary side wall and typical window to the nave.

Church of St. Mary East window.

West window.

The main north-west door leads into the porch and the main body of the church, revealing there a warm richness and an open aspect without the encumbrance of supportive pillars.

North west Door.

This particular design provides an excellent acoustic quality much valued to this day by visiting choirs and musicians performing in the church at special invitation.

Church interior.

Close by the Pulford church at the western end of the old Pulford Approach to the Eaton Estate there are two lodges or gatehouses that present interesting elements of pre-John Douglas design. They are constructed in large sandstone block with Dutch gable work supporting decorative ball elements. Windows are set in sandstone to mullion, lintel and sill whilst the wall at the North side lodge provides a fitting place for the Grosvenor coat of arms in cartouche.

Pulford Village School (1879) was renovated, with several additions, to a John Douglas design and although the school was sadly closed in July 1982 the building was later tastefully converted into three attached houses.

Pulford Village School. (recent photograph).

Many in Pulford village and beyond still fondly recall happy schooldays shared with their contemporaries many years ago. The building possessed a solid functionality relieved by vernacular addition. The pitched grey-slate roof had, on the ridge, an interesting four-sided bell- housing with a suggestion of gazebo shape. The roof interestingly incorporated a hip extension over a designated entrance door made from solid oak. High gables overhung half-timbered decorative divisions that incorporated white plaster panels suggesting the vernacular style of buildings on the Cheshire/Shropshire border. An interesting example of this vernacular style is still to be found in the Black & White cottages (1885-86) in the Poulton approach to the Eaton Estate. There the full black painted timber-work to upper and lower storey is, at times, forcefully strong and heavy and, as is usual, divided by a white plaster finish. The whole design perhaps is strongly basic and functional whereas the usual half-timbering appearing on the school and elsewhere is more finely balanced.

*The Black &
White Cottages
(Poulton
Approach).*

The main sandstone walls of the school conveyed a strong sense of worth and purpose, while the high windows having many small rectangular glass panes admitted light but inhibited pupil distraction from the outside world during lesson time. The main doors, with separate entrances for boys and girls, were both of solid construction and functional whilst the main playground was extensive. The whole appearance of the building conveyed something of the growing interest and concern for the useful education of the young which was part of the fashionable patronage of the nineteenth century and the passing of the 1870 Education Act.

The associated Schoolmaster's House (1895) possesses a skilful blend of country cottage style with some interesting decorative features identifying the architectural style of John Douglas. A Welsh slate roof carries a tall spiral chimney and a small dormer addition. The plain gable frontage is set above white half plastering which leads to a moulded brick string division separating the upper wall sections. Within this upper wall section are the upper storey windows set in substantial mouldings with larger glass panes than one might expect, and a series of decorative blue-brick diamond patterning to relieve the basic brickwork pattern. The lower storey repeats much of the above in balance, with the addition of strongly designed oak doors and larger windows.

The Schoolmaster's House.

The Victorian era was socially hierarchical and this was reflected in architectural differences. The Limes (1872) (now Green Paddocks) is an impressive three storey building described by Edward Hubbard as 'remarkable even among the Eaton Estate buildings for the care and expense lavished upon it' and consequently the original Estate tenant must have been specially favoured.

Green Paddocks Front elevation facing East

The red-tiled roof, from which tall, elegant chimney-stacks extend, is an extensive hip with a small, projecting pitched roof.

*Green Paddocks
(Gable Roof)*

At the front elevation there is a superb pargeted gable incorporating a Westminster initial motif. Here also are complex finial and moulded coping to the Dutch gables. Below each gable head a pleasing design of eight vertical, rectangular inlaid mouldings overhang four arched-head windows. These windows, as with others at the house, carry unusual leaded–light patterning. However perhaps the most impressive feature in the design is the brick moulding in the string courses, sills, mullions and carved heads and although much of the brick was apparently made locally much of the more intricate shapes in hardened brick may have been made in North Wales brickyards. Of further interest is the decorative frieze of moulded brickwork emphasising the division between the ground floor and upper storeys.

All around the house there are intricate mouldings, introduced windows and roof projections and shapes that convey architectural skill and variety and the best of workmanship.

Upper Levels.

The main door.

Window detail.

Southern aspect.

Indeed, it is true to say, that this house possesses a remarkable range of architectural features that demonstrates the capability and professional qualities of John Douglas.

The Grosvenor Pulford Hotel.

The Grosvenor Arms recently sensitively extended in the John Douglas style is now advertised as The Grosvenor Pulford Hotel, but was originally a farmhouse trading with an early public house licence under the name of 'The Talbot.' John Douglas was required to remodel the building (1887) and features identifying his design are still to be found in the main building.

The chimney-stacks present an interesting architectural feature in that they display complex rectangular brickwork panels below protective coping stones. Above the roof ridge the panels are in trio whilst on the pitch of the roof the panels are restricted to two but the brickwork is extended to the fourteen brick herring-bone design.

The main door is impressive being recessed in blocked stone that has suitable headstone lintel. Above the door is the Grosvenor heraldic display with a Latin inscription 'Virtus Non Stemma' possibly translated as (Worth not Birth) or literally Virtue not Family Pedigree.

Heraldic Device & Motto.

The windows having four or three leaded light panels have large panes by the main door in blocks of three by seven smaller panes. Looking carefully at the rainwater goods it is possible to detect a date (1897) on a downspout rose.

Grosvenor Pulford Hotel, (Window detail).

Brookside Farm house.

Many of the former farmhouses in Pulford and Poulton were remodelled to designs by John Douglas during the period of 'Estate Improvement' directed by the First Duke of Westminster in the latter half of the nineteenth century. Furthermore many of these traditional farms during the late twentieth century have been converted to family homes with the outbuildings being skilfully adapted and modernised as apartments and houses – 'barns to bedrooms' with much John Douglas architectural design being preserved.

Brookside Farm house (Gable detail)

Brookside Farm house, Pulford (1885-86) was designed as a complete farmstead similar in style to the Gorstella Farm at Gorstella - a small hamlet situated to the north-west of Pulford. Brookside Farm has a picturesque appearance in brick with 'stone for mullions and other dressings'. The elevations and gable heads are 'rather prettier' than at Gorstella as there is an elaboration of Dutch gable with curving support to end stone platforms providing potential for decorative ball or finial. The windows are now in large pane and the main door is suitably impressive with strong wood panel and original

The Elms house frontal.

ironwork in lock and hinge. The house is impressively set on an elevated former causeway above Pulford Brook, the political borderline between England and Wales.

The Elms. The typical John Douglas porch.

The Elms, Wrexham Road, Pulford (1871) at one time the residence of Captain David Scotland, the first Duke's secretary, is impressive in design. The roof is of red tile, now significantly weathered and softened in appearance. The chimney-stacks are tall to chimney pot with channelled

recess in the brickwork. Ridge tile is charmingly decorative in rounded open work reflecting to some extent the decorative hanging tile work on upper walls. The main gable is delightfully half-timbered whilst pitched roof projections from the main roof appear alongside. String coursing in rounded edge divides upper and lower storey. The main door is sited within an impressive porch which itself has a half-timbered frontal supported by solid oak corner posts firmly fixed on a sandstone base.

The Manor Farm House (1871 and later modification 1896-98) Wrexham Road, Pulford.

The Manor Farm house – Front of house view.

The house has an impressive appearance from the eastern side. The chimney stacks are brick built with some having a decorative channel in herring bone finish. The roof probably formerly of slate has apparently been replaced throughout in a reconstituted slate-like material. The twin front gables are typical John Douglas features having decorative ball head and subordinate repetition at the lower level edge.

The Manor Farm house – Porch.

The main house walls are of shaded local brick with solid stonework as surround to window lintel and sill holding clear pane work. The main door has a protective stone support and threshold and above the door a stone tablet incorporates a date (1896) and the Westminster (W) motif. The main outbuildings again reflect John Douglas style having a half- timbered design under a functional gable head with typical local brick-work incorporating moulded string-courses separating storey level. Windows and double doors are functional but present a balance and unity of design to the main building.

An additional dwelling to the western side (known as The Groom's House) is also of John Douglas design reflecting some of the described features of the main house.

Iron House Farm.

Iron House Farm (1884) Dodleston Lane is an imposing, functional building. The reference to Iron House would indicate a chosen building material for main supports to the house following industrial revolution design and theory. The John Douglas remodelling (1884) contains tall brick chimney-stacks with channel finishing, and the typical red tile roof. The front of the house facing Dodleston Lane is strongly indicative of John Douglas design – the walls are of quality red brick, with blue-brick diaper decorative finish, moulded stringing at storey level and with six windows of varying design to the widow pane pattern (see photograph). The front wall has a central section extension to include a main door and inner porch. The front door is of heavy oak and is positioned within a typical substantial light-coloured stone surround. Above the lintel in raised sandstone is a raised Westminster motif and the split date 1884. The main structure of the farmhouse continues the essential elements of the design to provide a substantial working farmhouse with some decorative relief. The single-storey extension at the rear of the farmhouse has a slate roof but appears to be a later addition with basic materials in window and door design.

Many of the cottages in Pulford were also designed or remodelled by John Douglas and the architectural characteristics of his design continue to enhance the appearance of the village.

*Park House/
Carden Cottage/
Ivy Cottage.*

Park House, Carden Cottage and Ivy Cottage (dated 1887) situated on Wrexham Road and within the village complex retain many examples of John Douglas design.

The spiral twist style chimneys, red tile roofs with distinctive Dutch gable outline, provide square end finish. The mullion windows within sandstone frame to sill and lintel provide for traditional diamond pattern pane-work. Other cottages within the village complex such as Brook House, Jasmine Cottage and Bank Cottage show some evidence of John Douglas stylistic reference with spiral chimneys remaining but there has apparently been extensive alteration and modification over the years.

Woodside Cottage.

Woodside Cottage (dated 1889) on Wrexham Road to the north side of the village is on the site of two older cottages but is now a single dwelling and a superb example of retained John Douglas cottage design. The distinctive features include the spiral chimney pattern, the red tile roof and the half-timber work at the twin gable heads. There is quality brick-work to the walls with decorative enhancement in the blue-brick diamond work and in the moulded stringings to storey level. The brick moulding to window surrounds and mullions support traditional diamond pane pattern, whilst below the windows the rectangular frieze of decorative diamond brickwork on pargeted base is a further distinctive feature.

The porch is centrally positioned to provide proportional unity to the detached building. The hip roof is of red tile supported by oak corner posts with brick- work base allowing for diamond- pane window work above where necessary. The main oak entrance door is positioned at the sheltered south side of this neatly designed porch.

Woodside Cottage (Porch)

The former Clerk of Works house at Cuckoo's Nest dated 1881 is now known as Clerkhouse and was originally the home and work place of the Clerk at the Cuckoo's Nest Estate yard where records and accounts were stored during the Grosvenor Eaton Estate development of the late nineteenth century. The house itself is in developed

The Clerkhouse.

cottage style and is interesting in its variety of material and design. High chimney-stacks are channelled to plain chimney pots of varying height and shape above a red tile roof with plain ridge tile having decorative triple-leaf end stops. The roof ridge is of a different height to accommodate an additional gable over the southern side. At the northern projection over the original front door there is an interesting semi-dormer window and roof space where children or a house servant may have had a room. There are impressive projections of heavy timber roof rafter and joist and some very early examples of pebble- dash rendering on the upper walling and around leaded light widow panes set in typical sandstone frame. Indeed the window frames around the house are largely sculptured sandstone to lintel, mullion, and sill with small square pane-work around an octagonal central pane that allows for unobstructed view. However this style is not always apparent as other windows to the south side are of moulded brickwork instead of sandstone and this raises some questions in relation to consistency of style.

Clerkhouse original front door.

The original front door now screened by the hedge from the Wrexham Road is of oak within a sandstone frame in long and short block placement to a decorative lintel that includes a triple-leaf design and preserved original date (1881).

Above this main door there is an interesting continuation of string-course brick in long and short work separating upper and lower storeys. The lower storey is built of common brick made at the Estate yard while the upper storey wall is finished in early pebble-dash render. The central upper and lower storeys project from the main wall, allowing additional space in the upper room, and are supported at the lower ends by strongly carved corbel supports while the centre width appears as built out brick. Above the central window and to the central gable there is a good example of nicely balanced half-timber work that includes a wooden framed triple casement window holding leaded light pane work.

Clerkhouse central window original front.

The original rear of the house, now the present front allows for easier access and car parking. Here the windows and doors follow similar designs again repeated at the southern aspect where the twin gable units create additional space.

Clerkhouse southern view twin gable.

The main outhouse is built of common brick with a red tile roof. There is an example of intersecting tracery work on an original metal window but other windows on this outbuilding appear to be recent replacements.

Clerkhouse outhouse (original window).

Edward Hubbard in 'The Work of John Douglas' refers to a pair of cottages (1872-76) to the west of Cuckoo's Nest on the road to Oldfield's Farm. One semi-detached pair of basic functional design (Poplar Cottage/Damson Cottage) has a red tiled roof, plain, strong, sandstone frame windows and good solid front doors which would indicate some stylistic reference to John Douglas basic design.

Poulton, the associated hamlet to Pulford village, contains some excellent examples of John Douglas architectural style in the farms, farm outbuildings, and in the cottages. However it must be reiterated that many of these buildings are no longer in traditional use often being converted to modern requirement as family dwellings.

Wallet's Farm house.

Wallet's Farm house is a very good example of a John Douglas rural building which incorporates many of the Victorian 'model farm' suggested improvements to the outbuildings and stock-yard plan. The farmhouse has the high spiral chimneys, Welsh slate roof, and attractive blue-brick diamond interlay to good local red brick walling. There is a nicely rounded string-course between storey level with a raised element above the front porch. Windows at lower level are set in moulded brick surround in banks of four with shaped heads above square pane work whilst upper storey windows are in wood frame. The porch roof is attractively shaped in slate and is supported by triangular frames above built in sandstone. The entire appearance of the farmhouse provides a sense of functional proportion and architectural balance.

Wallet's Farm outbuilding.

As viewed from Straight Mile the adjacent outbuilding is both functional and decorative. There is a plain slate roof extending over the length of the local red-brick building. Sensible provision has been made for air-brick above while the John Douglas design for the balanced window spacing below has been slightly but sensitively modified. This shippon accommodated dairy cattle stalls and a useful end meal house with provision for a hay store above with convenient feeding traps to stock below. During the mid- twentieth century internal adaptations have been made to comply with increased regulation and mechanisation. On this outbuilding John Douglas also provides compatible blue-brick diagonal finish whilst the blue-brick also provides balanced contrast at the level of the string-course.

Green Farm house presents a very well-maintained appearance with several recognisable John Douglas architectural features. The traditional red tiled roof accompanies the typical spiral chimneys supported on high stacks. The walls are of warm red brick in local variety with moulded string- courses at two levels. The ten windows are nicely spaced with a square single at third storey level, five evenly spaced rectangular windows at second storey, and two windows either side the main door at ground level. The heavy main door has two square windows at the topmost level to allow for additional light.

Green Farm house

Green Farm outbuildings.

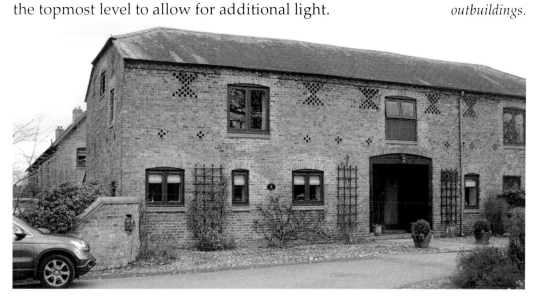

The Green Farm outbuildings have been converted to individual dwellings to modern specification and although the exterior appearance pleasingly continues a reference to John Douglas design with retained traditional slate roof, local red brick walling, and window frame pattern, painted to Grosvenor/Westminster red, the interiors contain all modernised improvements.

The Grange Farm house.

Grange Farm house (1896-98) presents a most impressive appearance within attractive landscape design and garden surround. There are many recognisable John Douglas design features including the elegant spiral twist chimneys set upon a traditional slate roof. There are nicely balanced small dormer windows in the main roof and the gable ends to the main roof have typical finial decorative finish. Local red brick to the upper walls contain typical blue brick pattern work in interesting relief. Windows are strongly framed in stone work to mullion, lintel and sill. The main doorway, from the driveway approach, presents a formidable appearance with protective porch in stone block surround under a pediment containing the Westminster initial motif in cartouche. The tasteful extension to the property incorporates many references to John Douglas design and is very much an integral part of the house.

Grange Farm house from driveway approach.

At the present time Yew Tree Farm House is undergoing some renewal and maintenance although the outbuildings which were remodelled by John Douglas (1885 – 86) and again after a fire in 1887 have been very recently separated from the farmhouse (2006 plan application) and have been extensively modernised subsequently to provide a series of impressive 'barn-type' dwellings.

Yew Tree Farm house.

Yew Tree Farm prior to conversion.

These apartments contain several references to John Douglas design: the red tile roof, the window framing in the red brick walling, and the half- timber gable work over the main doorway being the most evident.

Chapel House Farm is also about to undergo extensive renovation and has considerable history as an original farm. The oldest part of the house is reputed to be sixteenth century and may have been built following acquisition of Cistercian land subsequent to the Dissolution of the Monasteries. There is a date stamp on an outbuilding of 1868 suggesting a very early remodelling before John Douglas commission. On the north side of the house within a gable frontage there is a large letter W in outline brick that suggests reference to Westminster Estate. There is, however, no detectable reference to John Douglas design and any remodelling is likely to precede his work locally.

Chapel House Farm Cottages.

These cottages provide superb examples of John Douglas symmetrical cottage design. There are the cylindrical twisted chimneys on a shared chimney-stack upon a red tiled roof. The twin gable frontage is extensively decorated in blue brick diagonal above a moulded brick string-course. Upper storey triple windows are framed in moulded brick to lintel and sill and are replicated in lower storey where the walled brickwork is in variable red tone.

In conclusion it is apparent that the influence of John Douglas continues to provide both aesthetic and functional qualities to the architectural unity of Pulford and Poulton. There is much careful maintenance of the traditional buildings and where some of these buildings have had to be adapted or extended there has been an acknowledgement to the work of John Douglas in their sympathetic design. In addition new buildings in Pulford and Poulton often reveal certain John Douglas architectural characteristics in appropriate memorial to him and his excellent work.

Acknowledgements.

*Edward Hubbard 'The Work of John Douglas'
pub. The Victorian Society (1991).*

*Finally many thanks and much appreciation to all owner/
occupiers of the properties who have given permission
for photographs and who have provided so much helpful
assistance in support of this project.*

Chester and Wrexham Turnpike Trust

By Gaenor Chaloner

Local roads before the formation of the Chester and Wrexham Turnpike Trust were generally of very poor quality and badly maintained. To improve the situation it was decided through an Act of Parliament in 1761, '*to enlarge the term and power of an act of repairing. To repair and widen from Chester to Wrexham through Pulford and a lane called Wrexham Lane and Dee Bridge*'. The main Chester to Wrexham road which still travels through the centre of Pulford left Chester via the Old Dee Bridge which connected Chester with Handbridge and then went on to Wrexham. The Trust was formed and with the help of mortgages which were organised by the trustees to finance the project, together with the charges levied at the new tollgates, enabled improvements to be made to the quality of the road. The Trust also embraced some of the side roads which diverged from the main route to serve places such as Ffrith, Cefn y Bedd and Brymbo, which were important sources of coal, lime and other minerals. Prior to the Turnpike system being introduced, the roads were the responsibility of each parish for maintenance. They were often maintained by individual tenants who were held responsible to a limited degree for the maintenance to the road adjacent to their properties.

Notices were put in the local newspapers i.e.;
"Notice is hereby given that the Tolls arising and to be collected at the several Tollgates upon the Turnpike road from the city of Chester to Wrexham, in the County of Denbigh, called Two Mile House Gate and side gates; the Lavister Gate and Acton Smithy Gate and side gate; and also the Tolls arising and to be collected from Rossett bridge to Geggin Wen, in the counties of Denbigh and Fflint, or one of them called Cefn y Bedd, Ffrith and Brymbo Gates, will be let by auction, to the best bidder, for one year, from

the 1st day of January next at the Town Hall in the city of Chester."……. "Whoever happens to be the highest bidder must, at the same time, pay one month's rent in advance of the rent at which such tolls shall be let, and give security, with sufficient sureties, to the satisfaction of the Trustees, for the payment of the remainder of the money monthly."

Rossett railway station was built in 1846 by the Great Western Railway Company. The construction of the railway had a significant impact on the viability of the toll roads, as much of the business of moving heavy and bulky goods was transferred to the new form of transport. This is reflected in the Turnpike Trust's financial records. Revenue from the tolls appears to have broken even when taking into account the cost of the mortgages and rent arrears which did occur regularly. The Trust could not compete with the railway and it was proving to be not viable any more so it was decided to close down the Trust in 1877.

Postcard of Rossett Station c.1911 Courtesy of Audrey Gibson

Rossett Station.

On the closure of the Trust, all of the toll houses were surveyed before being put up for sale or demolished. The first part of the survey gives the following details:

No.1 Two Mile House, Township of Eccleston:
Occupied by Thomas Powell

This house projects about six feet on the side of the path and will no doubt have to be removed. It is surrounded by His Grace the Duke of Westminster's property which includes the garden of the property. The value of old materials, bricks, slates, 5 small windows, two gates, posts and pales, a lamp, a broken boiler, spouting in front of the house, oven and grate in living room and movable screen is £17. (in pencil in the margin is written, £15 offered on the presumption that the house is to come down).

No. 2 Rake Lane side gate and house, Township of Eccleston:
Occupied by John Jones

If this cottage is allowed to remain it will not be obstructive to the traffic. It is however a very unsightly poor dwelling. The pigstye belongs to the tenant. Value of the house if it is allowed to remain is £30. Value of old material if pulled down is £5. The site would have to go to the road. (in pencil is written £25 offered).

No.3 Lavister Gatehouse, Township of Allington:
Occupied by C. Richardson

This is a poor dwelling house with cow house and outbuildings. If allowed to remain it would be no obstruction to public traffic. The value of the house if allowed to remain with outbuildings, land, timber gate and fixtures is £140. If the house is taken down the value of the land, timber gate and fixtures will be £110. There are 3 Oak trees, 4 Ash trees and 3 Sycamore trees on this property. (in pencil is written M. Samuels offers £120).

The site on which Lavister Gatehouse stood (now occupied by the Gatehouse Veterinary Hospital)

The report goes on to describe the other Toll Gates on this road network which belonged to the Turnpike Trust namely: No.4, Cefn y Bedd old toll house; No.5, Cefn Y Bedd new toll house; No. 6, Ffrith toll house; No.7, Brymbo toll house and gate and finally No. 8, Acton Smithy toll gate.

The final meeting of the Chester and Wrexham Turnpike Trustees took place on the 27th April 1878, the toll houses having been either demolished or sold off. At their peak the Turnpike Trusts numbered over a thousand in England and Wales and made a great difference to the quality of the road systems but it was a slow process until the 19th century when engineers like Thomas Telford and John Loudon McAdam came on the scene. For instance the engineering work done by Telford on the Holyhead road reduced the journey times of the London mail from 45 hours to 27 hours and the speed of the coaches increased from 5-6 mph to 9-10 making a great difference for travellers' journeys.

The County Council of Cheshire took over the responsibility for our road system in 1889. The A483 from Chester to Wrexham which cut through the centre of Pulford was, in the mid to late 20th century, one of the busiest roads in the country and literally cut the village in half because of the volume of traffic. The road was so busy with heavy haulage plus the sheer volume of light traffic, it could easily take up to ten minutes to cross the road to enable someone to catch a bus. As a matter of fact many buses were missed because of the inability to cross the road in time. It is quite amazing that for years the village had no 30 miles an hour speed restrictions, even though the entrance to the school opened out onto this extremely busy main road. Speed restrictions were only introduced into Pulford after a very long and hard fight by the Parish Council in 2006. Unfortunately this came after the closure of the school and the building of a new bypass during the 1980s. This bypass became the new A483 and the road through the village became the B5445. It must be said that a combination of speed restrictions and the building of the by-pass has made a considerable difference to the village as it has become a lot quieter and easier to get around on foot and the village no longer has that barrier through the centre due to the sheer volume of traffic.

References:

Cheshire Record Office LTE 1/2, LTE 5, LTE 6.

The Military History of Pulford and Poulton

By Margaret Hughes

There have been five significant periods in the military history of Pulford and Poulton. Roman from the first until the beginning of the fourth century, Norman from 1066, the English Civil War 1642-1646, World War I, 1914-1918, and finally World War II, 1939-1945. However, the term military does not necessarily mean a large armed force, but the local landed gentry or Lord of the Manor's armed retainers, vassals and tenants banded together for their defence. The proximity of Pulford and Poulton to North Wales would have meant frequent raids from over the border; the Welsh being attracted to the fertile Dee Valley. Fighting and raiding would have been a way of life for the inhabitants of Pulford and Poulton until after the defeat of the Welsh in the fifteenth century.

The Romans

The Romans were probably the first major military force in the area of Pulford and Poulton. Chester approximately five miles away was an important Roman garrison town, at first home to the Second Legion and then the Twentieth Legion known as the Victrix. The Twentieth Legion was stationed in Chester until it was withdrawn from Britain in the fourth century. The local tribes along the Welsh border would not have peacefully accepted the Roman invaders and the Romans would have needed a constant visible presence. There are Roman artefacts in the area. Many pieces of tile, pottery and glass have been found at the 'Poulton Dig' and at several places in Pulford.

Centurion

The Roman road came out of Chester through Heronbridge, and there is now evidence of a road in the woods just north of Pulford Village probably going to a ford near the Pulford Bridge. This road would have been used to bring stone from the quarry at Ffrith for use in Chester some twelve miles away, and at times the traffic on the road would have necessitated military patrols. There also may have been a Roman military outpost at Pulford guarding the ford, on or near to what is now Castle Hill. The eighteenth century Turnpike to Wrexham follows some of this earlier Roman road.[1]

After the Roman withdrawal from Chester, the Dee Valley was still populated by short, dark haired people, known to the Romans as the Cornovii who were Celts. Around 600 AD, tall, fair haired Anglo-Saxons began to migrate from Mercia and to settle peacefully on the fertile lowlands of Cheshire; they were followed by the Vikings, Norse and a small number of Danes. The majority of the newcomers who settled in Cheshire however, were Anglo-Saxon, which explains Chester having a Mercian Anglo-Saxon Earl by 1066.[2]

The Normans

The Normans successfully invaded England in 1066; King Harold and most of the important Anglo- Saxon Earls and Thanes were killed at the Battle of Hastings. William, Duke of Normandy was crowned King of England in Westminster Abbey on Christmas Day in the same year. The Normans brought with them the hated feudal system, and their own laws and language which still affect our lives today.

There was fierce resistance to the Norman occupation, and it took more than four years before the country was brought under control. First there was rebellion in East Anglia and in Yorkshire where large areas of the countryside were deliberately destroyed by William I. This is now known as the 'Harrowing of the North'. In the winter of 1069-70 the people of Chester and Shrewsbury rebelled against the ruthless Norman rule, and William I, and his army came directly from Yorkshire into Cheshire laying waste most of the land, and as in Yorkshire, causing much hardship and starvation. Cheshire was finally defeated at the battle of Nantwich. Earl Edwin (Eardwine), the Anglo-Saxon Earl of Mercia and Chester whose wife was sister to the deceased King Harold, lost the Earldom of Chester and also the Manors of Poulton and Pulford; however he kept some of his other Cheshire properties indicating that he did not play an active part in opposing the Norman invasion or the later uprising of 1069.

William I gave the Earldom of Chester to Ghebold a Flanders Nobleman, who was one of his chief commanders. Ghebold had trouble with his lands in Flanders and returned there to protect his property, only to be captured and detained for a long period by his enemies. The Earldom was then given to Hugh d' Avranche whose mother was King William's sister, and he is now thought of as the first Earl of Chester. Hugh had sailed from Normandy with his father Richard d' Avranche and a large number of knights and armed retainers; one of these knights being Hugh Fitz Osbern. The new Earl of Chester made Hugh Fitz Osbern one of his chief commanders, and a wealthy man by giving him lands in Cheshire and manors and land in Leicestershire. The Earl also

*Earls of Chester
Coats of Arms*[3]

ordered castles to be built along the border with North Wales to try and control the continual raiding by the Welsh. One of these castles was to be built by Hugh Fitz Osbern at Pulford. The name Pulford coming from 'Pwll – marsh and Fford a crossing'. The Pulford Castle was built in the traditional Norman style, with a Motte (mound) on which a keep was built with a surrounding bailey and strong earthworks. It was strategically sited next to the Pulford Brook which acted as a moat on one side, and near to the ford to guard the road into Wales.

The castle may not have been involved in frequent hostilities, but its very presence must have subdued the local population and acted as a deterrent to the Welsh who raided across the border. Hugh Fitz Osbern became the first Baron of Pulford; he probably brought from Normandy with him his own loyal retainers some of whom would have been given land in return for their allegiance and military service. Pulford and Poulton are both included in William's survey of England in 1088, now known as the Doomsday Book; Poulton being more important with its larger population.

The Barony of Pulford continued through the family of Robert d' Pulford who was a descendant of Hugh Fitz Osbern until it was acquired by Robert d' Grosvenor when he married the rich heiress Joan d' Pulford. Robert d' Grosvenor who became the Baron of Pulford is an ancestor of the present Duke of Westminster.

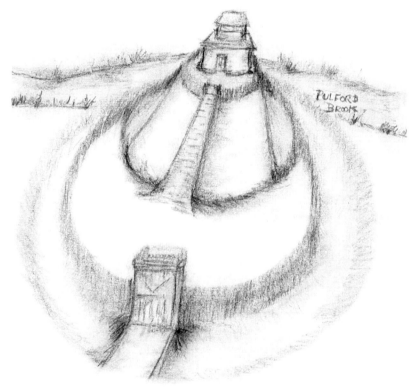

An example of a Motte and Bailey Castle

In the 12th century Pulford Castle and the other Marcher Castles were engaged in heavy fighting against the Welsh. Richard, the second Earl of Chester, and Henry 1st son, drowned in 1120 when the White Ship sank sailing from France, leaving Henry's daughter Matilda as heir. Some of the barons, not wanting a woman as the monarch, offered the throne to William 1st grandson, Stephen, thus starting a civil war. Ranulph, the third Earl of Chester, supported Stephen and then switched allegiance to the Empress Matilda. The Welsh took the opportunity during the Earl's absence to invade the Dee Valley, plundering, burning and laying waste to the land. The civil war was finally settled by compromise. Following King Stephen, Matilda's son Henry would inherit the throne, becoming Henry II, the first Plantagenet Monarch.

In 1402 King Henry IV ordered that all Marcher Castles be prepared for invasion by the Welsh under Owain Glyndwr. There was continual harassment and raiding until Owain Glyndwr was finally defeated. From then on Pulford Castle did not have a permanent garrison, and after Henry Tudor, who was Welsh, became Henry VII in 1485, there was no further trouble from Wales. By the 17th century Pulford Castle was in ruins.

Under the Normans and the early Plantagenets, England was at peace until the Lancastrians and the Yorkists differed over the rightful heir to the throne. Some of the local gentry may have supported one or other of the factions, but there was no military presence or fighting in the Pulford and Poulton area. This period is now known as the 'War of the Roses'. On August 22nd 1485, Henry Tudor claimed the English Crown after defeating Richard III of the Royal House of York at the battle of Bosworth, thus founding the Tudor dynasty.

The English Civil War

The English Civil War started in 1642 and by the end of the year there was a military presence in Cheshire, with troops in and around the Pulford and Poulton area.

Charles I had succeeded his father James I in 1625. James Stuart was James VI of Scotland having inherited the English throne from Elizabeth I, who was the last of the Tudor line. Charles' reign was complex, since his views and those of Parliament differed on the power of the monarchy. There were many problems with the religious differences in the country, and also over money and taxation. Charles at times could not agree with the MPs and had dismissed several parliaments. On January 4th 1642, Charles entered the House of Commons with an armed escort intending to arrest five members, John Pym, the Leader of the House being one of these MPs. However, having had prior warning, they were not present. Charles's action resulted in a ruling that all members were protected by Parliamentary Privilege and could not be arrested without the other MPs consent, a ruling still in force at the present time.[4]

Sir William Brereton. Courtesy of the Chester History and Heritage Centre

The situation rapidly deteriorated and in the early part of 1642 there was fighting in several parts of the country, and the people began to support either the King or Parliament. Later they began to identify the opposing sides, the Royalists as 'Cavaliers' and the Parliamentarians as 'Roundheads' because of the shape of the helmet worn by the parliamentary troops.

Sir William Brereton the MP for Cheshire was a Parliamentarian and the Commander in Chief of the parliamentary troops in Cheshire, making Nantwich his headquarters. By the end of 1642 Sir William Brereton's troops were in the area of Dodleston, Pulford and Poulton where they were garrisoned in the chapel at Poulton, which with its tower was an ideal military lookout. Sir William Brereton in 1646 sent letters to the troops in this area dated to within the last month of the surrender, referring to the need for strict guard at Poulton Green and the 'waterside at Poulton Hall', as the Royalists were smuggling provisions into Chester from Holt *'through Poulton and along the water to Eaton, sometimes they go through the fields betwixt Poulton and Pulford'*.[4]

St. Chad's Church Civil War Window – Farndon. Courtesy of the Rev. Capt. David Scurr

In 1643 he attacked the Royalist city of Chester without success as the Royalists held the bridge over the river Dee protecting the Bridge Gate into the city. The Royalists also held the bridge over the Dee at Holt and Farndon allowing support and supplies in from Royalist North Wales. On the 9th November 1643, Sir William Brereton and Colonel Thomas Mytton together with several thousand soldiers attacked the Holt and Farndon Bridge, defeating the Royalists with much slaughter and damage to property, and leaving the way open into North Wales. There were constant attacks on the Holt and Farndon Bridge by the Royalists until 1645, some of these led by Prince Maurice and Prince Rupert the King's nephews, and there was a constant movement of Parliamentarian and Royalist soldiers in and around the area of Pulford and Poulton, resulting in much hardship being suffered by the local people due to plundering by the troops.[4]

Charles I by Anthony Van Dyke
The Royal Collection @ 2010
Courtesy of Her Majesty Queen Elizabeth II

In May 1645 Sir William Brereton's soldiers were withdrawn from attacking Chester to protect central Cheshire from the threat of attack by troops from the Royalist garrison at Llangollen. The Parliamentarians retreated from the city and crossed the river Dee at Eccleston as the bridge at Chester was still held by the Royalists. Some of these soldiers made their way from Eccleston through the fields to Pulford where they grazed their horses while they went swimming in the Pulford Brook. Unfortunately for them, they were surprised by a party of Royalists led by a Colonel Trevor from Marford, who captured forty horses, eight men, their weapons and no doubt their clothes. The remaining Parliamentarians ran into Pulford Church, and Colonel

Trevor and his men only had to wait for them to come out and surrender. A 17th century church must have been a rather cold place for the wet and naked soldiers.

Sir William Brereton resumed the siege of Chester in June 1645, and his troops completely surrounded the city and out into the countryside around Pulford and Poulton. In December of that year he began a heavy bombardment of the city, and by January the citizens and soldiers were starving and could hold out no longer. On the 3rd February 1646, the Royalist Lord John Byron negotiated the surrender of Chester to Sir William Brereton. On May 5th 1646, King Charles surrendered at Southall to parliamentary forces, and on 30th January 1649, Charles Stuart, Charles I of England was executed at Whitehall, London, by order of a parliament under Oliver Cromwell.[4]

The civil war was over for the people of Chester and Pulford and Poulton, but it was a difficult time. Chester was partly in ruins and the surrounding countryside was stripped bare of crops and livestock. People had to try and rebuild their lives and live peacefully once more with those who may have supported the other side.

Returning once more to the military presence in Pulford and Poulton, in the Parish register for 1644 there is a record of a Richard Lee, a soldier in Colonel Washington's regiment being buried in Pulford churchyard. Colonel Washington was probably Colonel Henry Washington, a Royalist, who was a descendant of Sir William Washington of Northampton and of the same family as George Washington, the first President of America.

After the English Civil War there was a period of peace, although there were several changes of monarch. When Queen Anne, who was of Stuart descent, died leaving no heir, the Crown passed to the Elector of Hanover who became George I. During this time there was an unsuccessful invasion from Scotland by Charles Edward Stuart, 'Bonnie Prince Charlie'. His supporters were those who opposed the Hanoverian rule. Apart from this failed attempt to restore the Royal House of Stuart, there were no military troubles or fighting in Poulton and Pulford or any other part of the country. However the army was active on the continent and also in Canada and America.

Cheshire Yeomanry

The Cheshire Yeomanry was a light cavalry volunteer regiment raised in 1779 by Sir John Fleming Leicester. The word yeomanry; coming from yeoman, a small landowner or a country gentleman. The Cheshire Yeomanry was initially known as Sir John Fleming Leicester's Cavalry, and was formed for the purpose of defence should the country be invaded by French Napoleonic troops. All across the country other counties also raised volunteer regiments.

Thomas and Herbert Partington. Cheshire Yeomanry Uniform ca. 1900 Photograph courtesy of Anne Fair

In 1803 the regiment was re-formed and became the Earl of Chester's Regiment of Cheshire Yeomanry. In the same year the Prince Regent, later to become George IV, granted the regiment the privilege of using his crest, the 'Prince of Wales Feathers' on its badge. This badge has been proudly worn from that date until the present time. During the 19th century the regiment was made up of troops of approximately sixty men. In 1893 the troops were renamed squadrons, one of which became the 'B' (Eaton) Squadron, made up of volunteers from the area around Chester including many men from Pulford and Poulton, following on from the strong connection which the Grosvenors had with the regiment.

After the defeat of Napoleon Bonaparte and his army at the Battle of Waterloo, there was no further threat of invasion from the French. The country was peaceful apart from discontent and public disorder in the textile towns of Northern England. The Cheshire Yeomanry and other volunteer regiments were used by the local authorities to control the riots. Later the newly formed police took over civic control duties, allowing the regiment to return to its original purpose helping in the defence of the country at home, overseas duty was not obligatory for volunteer regiments.

In 1900 with trouble in South Africa, the Imperial Yeomanry was formed out of several regiments, including the Cheshire Yeomanry. Two companies of the Cheshire Yeomanry sailed for South Africa to what was called the 'Boer War'. One of its officers was Captain Lord Arthur Grosvenor, and with him probably went most of the Eaton Squadron. The Cheshire Yeomanry's first Battle Honours were awarded after the South African Campaign.

Sergeant Major John Tilston Moore
The stars on the uniform sleeve
denote years of service

Willam Moore
Cheshire Yeomanry dress
uniform

Photographs courtesy of Anne Fair

Local records from the 19th century show that there was an annual subscription of £10 to ride with the Eaton Squadron. However some of the troopers who were workers or tenants on the local estates would not have been able to afford this amount, and it is highly likely that the estate owners subsidized them. There was an allowance for uniforms of £3 per year for the first three years, all of which could be paid in the first year if necessary. Horses may have come from the stables of the local landowners or were an individual's riding or carriage horse. Older residents of Pulford and Poulton and Cuckoo's Nest remember the troopers parading and camping in the local area. The regiment camped at Eaton for annual training six times from 1911.

After the 'Boer War' and before 1914, the country had commercially and industrially expanded and had also acquired a large overseas Empire. Many European countries resented this success, but none more so than Germany.

The British Royal Family was of German descent and up to this time relations between the two countries had been cordial. However Kaiser Wilhelm II who was Queen Victoria's grandson was jealous of Britain, having his own ambitious plans for German expansion in Europe and overseas in Africa. Kaiser Wilhelm II had respected and been fond of Queen Victoria, but after her death and without her restraining influence on him the situation deteriorated.

The First World War

World War I was the first war fought on land, in the sea and in the sky. It began in 1914, when the countries of Europe being nervous of Germany's military expansion had been in an arms race for a number of years. Russia, France and Britain were united in the 'Triple Entente', with the German and Austro–Hungarian Empires in the 'Dual Alliance'; Belgium remaining neutral.[5]

On June 28th 1914 the heir to the Austro–Hungarian throne, Archduke Franz Ferdinand and his wife were assassinated in Sarajevo, Serbia. This incident had a knock on affect; the Austro–Hungarians declared war on Serbia, Russia defended Serbia, and so Germany on August 1st invaded France, Russia's ally, passing through neutral Belgium. This brought Britain into the conflict on August 4th 1914.

Nurses on steps of the Eaton Hall Estate Military Hospital 7 (Photograph CRO DDX 507 7)

A Day at Chester Races. Lady Arthur Grosvenor, nurses and wounded soldiers. Note the soldier sitting wearing a German cavalry helmet. (Photograph CRO DDX 507 8)

From August onwards, the young men including those from the Pulford and Poulton area volunteered for the armed forces. The Cheshire Yeomanry set up a tent in Rake Field, Rake Lane, Eccleston, where men could enlist. Many from this area volunteered in Rake Field, although at a later date they were transferred to other regiments. In happier times this field had been where the yeomanry had held several of its summer camps. In 1916 due to the large number of fatalities in France, conscription was started, also in the same year the yeomanry was sent to Palestine to fight against the Turkish Army. Captain Lord Arthur Grosvenor sailed with the regiment, while Eaton Hall, the Grosvenors' home, became a military hospital presided over by Lady Arthur Grosvenor. Many British and Empire soldiers were nursed there.

Injured soldiers at the Eaton Hall Estate Military Hospital (Photograph CRO 507 9)

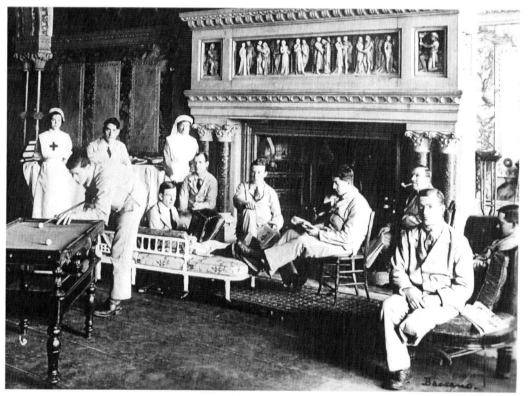

In 1914 the population of the Pulford and Poulton area was quite small and there were only seventy five men eligible for military service. Fourteen died, thirteen rest in France and Flanders, and one died of his war wounds at home on the 19th November 1918. In 1919 the local community wanted to have a special memorial to honour these men. The appropriate site was a small plot in front of what is now the Pulford Village Hall, but at that time was the Men's Reading Room, where they had probably spent many happy hours relaxing and enjoying the company of their friends and their neighbours. Pulford is probably quite unusual in having two war memorials, one in the grounds of St. Mary's Church, and the second one in front of the village hall, which was paid for by subscription raised locally. This memorial was unveiled in February 1920 by Lord Arthur Grosvenor at a service attended by the families of the deceased and local people from the surrounding area.

The inscription reads:

> *'Erected by the parishoners in grateful memory of the*
> *men of the parish who sacrificed their lives during the*
> *Great War, 1914 – 1918. They died that we might live'.*

Charles Broadhurst	Alfred Davies	Edward Edwards
Richard Broadhurst	James Davies	Cecil Griffiths
Harry Gibson	Joseph Davies	Bertie Jones
Ernest Leech	Thomas Davies	Joseph Probin
John Stockton	Ernest Thelwell	

1939 – 1945
William Valentine Woodall

At the end of World War I, the 'War to end all Wars', Pulford and Poulton like the rest of Britain had lost many of its young men and life was difficult. Unfortunately, the peace was short lived with unrest in Europe during the 1930's. This culminated in Hitler's Germany invading Poland on 1st September 1939. The next day Britain and France demanded Germany's withdrawal but were ignored. So on 3rd September, Britain along with France, Australia and New Zealand declared war on Germany.

Pulford War Memorial. Pulford villagers November 11th 2009

The Second World War

World War II began on September 3rd 1939 and the British Expeditionary Force sailed for France to help the French who were threatened by a German invasion. On May 14th 1940, the German tank regiments smashed through the Allies' front line and there was continual heavy fighting as the British and Allied troops fell back through Northern France towards Dunkirk on the French coast. After the evacuation from Dunkirk, the country's only protection was the Royal Air Force which was only one third of the size of Germany's. This is known as 'The Battle of Britain'.[6]

Supermarine Spitfire. Formerly of 610 Squadron, now restored and flying in the USA
Photograph courtesy of Michael Lewis

The building of planes and the training of pilots became the top priority. Hawarden over the border in North Wales four miles from Pulford and Poulton was a Royal Air Force base and a government sponsored 'Vickers' aircraft factory. By 1941 Hawarden was so busy that a satellite airfield was built at Poulton.[6]

Once again this brought a military presence into the Pulford and Poulton area. There were approximately 1,000 airmen and 100 airwomen split between Poulton and Hawarden airfields, causing heavy traffic on the country roads and noise from low flying planes overhead.

The Poulton Airfield was built mainly on the Duke of Westminster's Eaton Estate in the regular pattern of three runways in a triangle, with a slight bend in one of the runways to avoid Poulton Hall Farm. The runways and infrastructure were completed by George Wimpey & Co. There was a two storey control tower and at first just eight 'blister' hangars. There were no permanent hangars built as all the servicing was done at Hawarden. The airfield was sited between the Belgrave Avenue and the Pulford Approach (entrance to Eaton Hall) which was split into two; the main entrance was at the cut-off on the Pulford Approach on the straight mile, where many of the operational buildings were situated, and the living quarters and dining messes were all in the vicinity of Yewtree and Chapelhouse Farms.

Spitfire and Crew at Hawarden Airfield Photograph courtesy of Paddy Dalzell

The pilots who came to the Poulton Airfield were from many countries. They flew Oxfords, Mustangs, Hurricanes Spitfires, and at a later date Blenheims. Their training included practising bomb dropping at Fenn's Moss near Whitchurch, and air-to-ground firing at the Prestatyn Ranges on the North Wales coast, also landing planes in bad weather or poor visibility 'on the Beam' which was flying blind using directional radio signals.

WAAFs sitting on an Air Raid Shelter   *Crew sitting on a Mustang Aircraft*

Photographs courtesy of Nancy Bolton

Corporal Nancy Bolton was stationed at Poulton from 1943 onwards and has many memories of her time at the airfield. She was an aerial photographer who loaded the films into the planes and also removed and developed the films. She spoke of pilots from many countries and their enthusiasm for flying, and some of the things they did such as buzzing St. Mary's Church, Pulford when they took off, which was strictly against regulations. The sergeants on the base had rowing competitions on the River Dee against the naval personnel of equivalent rank who were at Eaton Hall with the naval cadets. The pilots also fined each other for flying mistakes such as landing badly, keeping what was known as the 'sin bin'. When this was full they then spent the money at the Grosvenor Arms Pulford, or at the Grosvenor Arms Aldford. Nancy remembers these young pilots 'living life to the full', and their dedication to duty.

By 1945 the airfield only had maintenance Royal Air Force staff and in 1957 the land reverted back to the Duke of Westminster and the adjoining farms; the control tower and all the buildings on the site were removed and now only the runways remain. While the Eaton Estate had the airfield on it, Eaton Hall apart from the 'private apartments and gardens' became a military hospital and from late 1942 was home to the Royal Naval College after the college buildings at Dartmouth were bombed and badly damaged. The Naval College was at Eaton Hall until 1946. The hall and accommodation was then used by the army as an officer cadet training unit until 1958.

Flight E seated in front of a Mustang
Photograph courtesy of Nancy Bolton

Pictures of a crashed Mustang Aircraft at Eaton Hall
Photograph courtesy of the Grosvenor Family Archive

Apart from all the activity at the Poulton Airfield and the Eaton Estate, the villagers of Pulford and Poulton were experiencing their own war. Many were in the armed forces or working long hours in the 'Vickers' aircraft factory at Hawarden and in the munitions factory in Chester; others had been drafted into 'important war work' including coal mining at the collieries just over the border in North Wales. The local farmers, while being urged to produce as much food as possible, were short of labour until 1943 when the 'Land Girls' first appeared, and many worked on the Pulford and Poulton farms. German and Italian prisoners of war were similarly employed.

There was also the Home Guard, although the headquarters were in Dodleston at the 'Primitive Methodist Chapel' which is now the Dodleston Village Post Office. The Home Guard mobile anti-aircraft guns were regularly on the 'Church Bank' (church car park), and there was ammunition and munitions stored in military lorries in the woods north east of Pulford and Poulton, with armed sentries on patrol.

At this time there were constant bombing raids over the Liverpool docks and Birkenhead, where there was shipbuilding, and some German planes leaving Merseyside dropped their remaining bombs over the Pulford area. Fortunately none of these bombs did any major damage, although one local farmhouse had a lucky escape. Local resident and former Mayor of Chester, Gerry Fair witnessed the crash at his home, Brookside Farm, when he was seventeen years old. He recorded this in his memoirs:

"The plane was a Junkers Ju 88 and I still have some parts of it, which were loaned to the Grosvenor Museum in 1988. I was standing on the lawn at Brookside about 10pm on 2nd November 1941, watching the raid on Merseyside. It was, of course, dark but quite cloudy, and because the searchlights were reflecting on the cloud this tended to make it appear quite like a bright moonlight. I became aware of a German plane flying West to East just below the cloud. As far as I could see there was nothing wrong with it. It appeared to pass right overhead, all of a sudden, the engine opened up to

a roar and then it started to dive flat out towards me. It hit the ground at great speed in the field we call Pheasant Field about 400 yards from where I was standing and blew into thousands of pieces most of which seemed to be on fire.

The nearest pieces fell behind the farm about 100 yards away and I must say that it made my heart miss a beat. At that point no one knew exactly what had happened. We did not know whether there were any unexploded bombs, but care had to be taken because there was a large fire where it had actually hit the ground and ammunition was exploding. We did not know whether any of the crew had parachuted to safety, but open parachutes were found, hence the rumour and the search by the Home Guard. Father rang for the Home Guard to turn out and, as we walked a little nearer to the plane through the smaller fires, people started to come in droves to see what had happened. Very quickly the police and the army arrived to control the crowd and keep them back from the area.

Junkers Ju 88 aircraft crashed at Brookside Farm. Photograph courtesy of Pulford & Poulton Local History Group

But, of course our family had a grandstand view. I cannot remember what time we got to bed, but by the time we left the scene, it was decided that there were no unexploded bombs, and that all of the aircraft's crew were dead, and the fires were more or less out. Just a group of soldiers were left to guard the plane.

Next morning we were up at the crack of dawn, an early breakfast and off across the fields to witness a scene of utter destruction. It was clear that the plane had flown straight into the ground..... There were pieces of body and clothes all over the field and on the hedge....(and) a strange green dye that spread all over the fields. (This was a dye that was used to help rescue aircraft that fell into the sea.)"

Gerry Fair.

BURIAL OF GERMAN AIRMEN

THREE RAID VICTIMS

Six pilot-sergeants of the Royal Air Force bore to the grave yesterday the remains of three of the German airmen who raided this country last Saturday night. The remains were all in one coffin, which bore a metal plate with their names. The victims had crashed in flames after being furiously attacked.

There must have been a fourth member of the crew, but no trace of him could be found.

The coffin draped in a Swastika flag of scarlet black, and white, bore a wreath of white and bronze chrysanthemums provided by the bearers. As the bearers emerged from the mortuary attached to the cemetery carrying their burden an R.A.F. officer stood at the salute before joining the procession to the graveside. The Vicar of the parish conducted a brief burial service.

The Second World War ended on the 3rd June 1945 in Europe and on the 2nd September 1945 in the Far East, when the Japanese surrender was announced. The people of Pulford, Poulton and Cuckoo's Nest together with the rest of the country were able to celebrate peace and look forward to happier times, and to the return of those who had been in the armed forces. All the young men and women who had been in 'uniform' were to come home safely, except sadly for one young man who is named on the Pulford Village Memorial. He was Sergeant William Woodall, a navigator flying in Wellington Bombers with the 70th Squadron; his plane was shot down over the Balkans in 1944, and his final resting place is in a communal military grave in Belgrade which was then in Yugoslavia.

Pulford and Poulton through the centuries have always had a strong military presence, opposing any invaders from the Romans and Normans onwards, repelling the constant raiding by the Welsh and, as Bowmen, serving the Earls of Chester. The courage of the people during the siege of Chester in the English Civil War should not be forgotten, nor should that of the Cheshire Yeomanry and, more recently, the famous 'Cheshires' which, as a regiment, no longer exists.

In Chester and the surrounding area there are many war memorials and cemeteries with war graves, poignant reminders of the sacrifices made by ordinary people, sacrifices which have been ongoing in numerous conflicts since 1945.

Acknowledgements.

Michael Lewis

Emma Stuart

Nancy Bolton

Paddy Dalzell

Mike Emery, Archaeologist, Poulton Dig

Caroline Mannion, Cheshires Military Museum, Chester Castle

Capt. R.C. Naylor, Chairman, Cheshire Yeomanry Association

Elizabeth Royles, Keeper of Early History, Grosvenor Museum Chester

Clare Carr, Assistant Curator, Cosford R.A.F. Museum

Liz Prescott

References

1   "Summary of Roman Roads", S.O. Dowyer

2, 3   "Barons of Pulford", Sir G, R, Sitwell, kindly loaned by Gaenor Chaloner

2, 3   "Cheshire Antiquities", Charles Hulbert, kindly loaned by Audrey Gibson

3   "Norman Earls of Chester", B.A.C. Husain

2, 3   "History of Cheshire", Dorothy Sylvester

3, 4   "Treasures of Cheshire", N.W. Civic Trust text N. Bilsborough

4   "The English Civil War Day by Day", Wilfrid Emberton, loaned by Gaenor Chaloner

5   "World War I", Stuart Ross

6   "World War II", Hermann Black

6   "Action Stations 3 Military Airfields of Wales and the North West", D.J. Smith.

6   "What did you do in the War Deva", Chester History and Heritage, Edited Emma Hart

7   Cheshire Records Office DDX 507

8   Cheshire Records Office DDX 507

9   Cheshire Records Office DDX 507

Centurion on page 77 courtesy of 'iStockphoto'

Parish of Poulton and Pulford Farm Holdings

By Tom Walker

The year 1919 was a very memorable one for the community of Poulton and Pulford. Until that year the village had been within the Eaton Estate, but a decision was taken by the estate to sell most of their properties on the western side which bordered Denbighshire and Flintshire, from Bretton to Pulford. 84 properties were auctioned by Knight Frank & Rutley at the Grosvenor Hotel, Chester on 1 February 1919. The 2nd Duke of Westminster was anxious to give his tenants every opportunity to buy their properties if they wished and this resulted in a tenants' syndicate being formed, chaired by Mr T R Probert of Bretton to negotiate the purchase of their farms. In total, some 6,000 acres were purchased by the tenant farmers. The total acreage sold was 7,376 comprising 55 farms, 26 smallholdings, the Grosvenor Arms Pulford and 148 cottages, including farms and cottages in this parish.

The properties had been built in the 1800s to the highest standards, many designed by John Douglas and the farmhouses often accommodated a "cheese factory." The size and quality of the workmanship has made them very desirable homes for the 21st century. Most properties have had several changes of ownership since that time, but notable exceptions are the Moore family from Iron House Farm who came in 1901, the Fair family who came to Brookside Farm in 1919 and the Edge family who came to Meadow House Farm in 1924, all of whom still farm in the parish in 2010.

Prior to World War II there were 22 farms in the parish varying in size from a few acres to several hundred acres. The farming was livestock based, the most popular breed of cattle being shorthorns. The milk was used for fresh milk sales and cheese making. Some farms grew arable crops for on-farm use.

Shorthorn cattle at Green Farm, Poulton

Much of the milk produced was used for cheese making and there was fierce competition between the cheese makers to produce the best cheese. Extra pennies could be gained if a cheese gained top marks at the local Cheese Fairs. These were held at Chester, Nantwich and Whitchurch during the grass-growing period which extended from spring to autumn. Each year a cheese made by the Mullock family at Poulton Hall Farm was presented to the owner of the horse winning the Chester Cup at the May race meeting until cheese production ceased in the mid 1930s.

Milk not used in cheese making was put in 17 gallon churns and taken by the farmer to either Rossett or Balderton stations to be put on a train to Co-op Dairies and others on Merseyside. Having a good fast horse and sound milk float to beat your neighbour avoided the queue!

In 1933 the Milk Marketing Board was formed and transformed the dairy industry. Instead of farmers having to find their own markets for their milk and collect payment the MMB bought the milk wholesale, paid the farmers and organised the marketing of it into liquid milk sales or dairy processing companies.

Cheese-making at Green Farm Poulton, home of the Denson family

In the late 1930s the threat of another war was looming. At that time Britain was importing 70% of its human food requirements and a considerable amount of animal food. A Wartime Agricultural Committee was set up and instructed farmers to plough a percentage of pasture to grow corn for human food and root crops such as turnips to feed the animals thus reducing the need to import these commodities. The committee had the power to evict farmers who didn't comply with the scheme.

A root crop being collected for winter feed to be stored in a hogg

Throughout Britain two million extra acres of pasture were ploughed up under this scheme often referred to as the "Plough Up Campaign". In addition, the need to produce more food created the "Dig for Victory" campaign which encouraged people to grow vegetables in gardens and allotments. Farm labour became scarce at this time as young men were called up into National Service. In 1939 the Women's Land Army and Timber Corp was formed to undertake work normally carried out by men. Some worked on farms in this parish and lifelong friendships were formed. Their contribution to the war effort was finally recognised in 2009 when the surviving members were presented with a commemorative medal.

During the war, in order to increase food production the government imported tractors from the USA and supplied them to large farms and farm contractors under the Lease-Lend scheme to gradually replace horses which meant new skills had to be learned. The pictures below feature the Allis Chalmers Model B fitted with a mowing machine at Brookside Farm Pulford and the other photograph is of a McCormick W12 pulling out of Yew Tree Farm, Poulton. Both these tractors were imported from America under the Lease-Lend scheme.

Farmers' wives and farm workers' wives were also employed and often babies in prams and young children were brought to the shippon while their mothers milked the cows. Another wartime enterprise was rearing of poultry which gave some wives the opportunity to sell chickens and eggs at the door. In some cases this work replaced their previous job of cheese making. Many people who had suitable outbuildings kept pigs, the principle being one for the family and one for the Ministry of Food to be distributed throughout the nation. Animal food was rationed in the same way as human food. Pig keeping was carried on after the war using the Nissen Huts at the Yew Tree Farm campsite until 1963. At that time, Yew Tree Farm, Poulton was owned by the Liverpool Co-operative Society Ltd. and to celebrate the end of the war the Society organised a visit to their factory for the staff of Yew Tree Farm. The programme of events is listed below.

LIVERPOOL   CO-OPERATIVE   SOCIETY   LTD.

Farm Staff visit to L. C. S. Factories
Friday, June 22nd, 1945.

PROGRAMME

3-15 p.m.	Coach leaves Yew Tree Farm for Lockerby Road.
4-15 p.m.	Visit Dairy and Confectionery Bakery.

5-15 p.m.	Tea at Confectionery Bakery.
6-0 p.m.	Coach to Royal Court Theatre.
6-15 p.m.	Attend performance of "Miss Hook of Holland".
8-30 p.m.	Coach to Unity House Cafe.
8-45 p.m.	Supper and Speeches at Cafe.
10-0 p.m.	Coach leaves Cafe for Yew Tree Farm.

YEW TREE FARM NOTES

Total Land	720 acres.
Land Ploughed	84 acres.
Stock	340 Dairy Cows, 62 Calves, 4 Bulls, 20 Pigs, 2 Horses.
Milk Produced	week ended June 16th approx. 4000 gallons.
Staff	14 full - time, 6 part - time.

In addition to farm land being ploughed up for additional crops in the early 1940s, Grosvenor Estate land in Poulton was requisitioned to build an airfield. This affected four farms, Poulton Hall, Green Farm, Yew Tree Farm and Chapel House Farm. Poulton Hall was left with only a very small acreage to farm but this was supplemented with land at Bridge Farm, Kinnerton. The airfield came into operation on 1st March 1943.

After the war ended, the mechanical revolution forged ahead with tractors becoming more readily available and new farming techniques began to emerge. Henry Ford and Harry Ferguson had the greatest influence at the time. Harry Ferguson developed the "Ferguson System", the ability to carry an implement on the rear of the tractor and so transfer its weight to the rear wheels of the tractor to improve its traction.

This Hydraulic Lift System invented by Harry Ferguson was recently voted (in a Farmer's Weekly Poll) the greatest innovation to mechanization in the last 75 years. Meadow House Farm on Dodleston Lane bought a petrol version in 1948 for the princely sum of £247.0s.0d. The tractor and its attachments took over many tasks previously done by horses thereby reducing the physical work of the labour force and speeding up production.   The tractors of this era were powered by petrol and TVO (tractor vaporising oil). The engine was started with petrol and when sufficiently hot, manually switched to TVO. The next step in modernisation was the introduction of tractors fuelled by diesel which produced more power and enabled larger implements to be used.   Haymaking was transformed from pitchfork to pick-up baler and corn harvesting from threshing machine to combine harvester.

During the 1950s an important development relating to cattle health was the introduction by the Ministry of Agriculture of testing cattle for tuberculosis and any cattle found to carry the disease were slaughtered and compensation given to the farmer.   Also at this time new regulations required cattle housing to have cement rendered interior walls, metal cow stalls with increased light and ventilation before a Tuberculin Tested Licence would be issued to allow milk production to continue.

A further development was the growing use of artificial insemination of dairy cattle which gave farmers greater opportunities to select the genetics of their herd and improve the quality of their cows and quantity of milk production. At this time the breed of dairy herds was usually either Shorthorns or Ayrshires but Friesians, initially imported from Holland, soon became the popular choice for most farmers due to their greater milk yield.

In addition to dairy farming, poultry farming was also a feature of the parish. Mr Edward Eckford of Oldfields Farm, Cuckoos Nest, had a hatchery producing day-old chicks alongside his dairy enterprise until he sold the farm to Mr R D Wilson in 1958. It continued as a dairy farm but also a large turkey unit was established as the annual Christmas treat had become more affordable. The finished birds were taken to J. P. Woods of Craven Arms to be dressed and marketed but with falling profit margins production ceased in 1973.

Poultry rearing at Brookside Farm

In the early 1960s Lyndale Farm initially produced broiler chickens for a growing population enjoying a better standard of living and who consumed white meat on a regular basis. Later the farm produced   eggs for broiler chicken production. The eggs were taken to a hatchery near Frodsham. Also in the 1960s an egg retailing business was set up at Siglen Cottage under the name 'Today's Egg & Poultry'. Now large-scale poultry and egg production is no longer carried out in the parish.

The sixties was also a time of change in the dairy industry. Silage was rapidly taking the place of hay due to its greater nutritional value for milk production and its less weather dependent harvesting. The National Agricultural Advisory Service (NAAS) was set up to advise farmers on new technology and help them take advantage of Grant Aid to build new facilities for the housing, feeding and milking of dairy cows.

 Mr Hywel Evans of Saltney designed a cubicle housing system to replace the traditional shippon. It allowed the cows greater freedom of movement and access to silage during the wintertime. This   system of housing was adopted at Brookside Farm, Pulford during the winter of 1963. NAAS organised an Open Day at Brookside farm to promote the benefits of this new system. The milking system itself also changed with cows being milked in a herringbone parlour and the milk going directly by pipeline to a large tank in the dairy, and then collected by a bulk milk tanker and taken to a local dairy.

This period of rapid progress was temporarily halted in October 1967 when foot-and-mouth disease devastated the dairy industry throughout Cheshire. Eleven farms in this parish were affected resulting in the loss of 1,164 cattle, 497 sheep and 37 pigs. The last outbreak in Cheshire which was a re-infection occurred at Rake Farm, Eccleston on Easter Sunday, 7 April 1968.

To help farmers re-stock their farms after foot-and-mouth, the National Farmers Union, agricultural auctioneers and cattle breed societies formed registers of available cattle. Farmers travelled far and wide to buy replacement stock, some as far as Canada to buy Canadian Holstein Friesians. Foot-and-mouth restrictions were finally lifted on 8th May 1968.

Wallets Farm Foot-and-Mouth Fire.
A familiar scene at this time.
Courtesy of Liverpool Daily Post

In 1974, in conjunction with the Cheshire Agricultural Society and NAAS, grassland demonstrations were staged at Poulton Hall Farm, Green Farm and Chapel House Farm to show different types of machinery available for silage making. NAAS has now become the Agricultural Development and Advisory Service (ADAS). The Cheshire Show was held at Poulton Hall Farm and Green Farm for two consecutive years but access problems caused it to be moved to Tatton Park, Knutsford and then to Tabley where it has a permanent site. The farming of the seventies and early eighties had been a period of continuous expansion. Improved grassland management, artificial fertilisers and more powerful machinery increased farm output. However, farmers were to become the victims of their own success when in 1984 the European Union, which the United Kingdom had joined in 1973, introduced quotas to control production in an effort to reduce surplus commodities which had built up. One of the effects of this policy rendered smaller farm units uneconomical as their potential output was limited.

In 1981 the Grosvenor Estate built a new dairy unit (Park Farm) utilising the concrete runways of the disused wartime airfield at Poulton. The land had been part of Green Farm, Poulton but when the Denson family retired the farm was not re-tenanted. The buildings were then used as a calf rearing unit by Mr Barry Faulkner. These buildings have since been developed into desirable homes.

As farmers retired, their land has been absorbed into other farms, creating larger units which are able to benefit from the economies of scale. The buildings at Grange Farm, Pulford became part of the extension of the Grosvenor Pulford Hotel and Iron House Farm buildings became part of the Bell Meadow housing development in Pulford. In Poulton, Green Farm buildings were developed into six residential properties.

More recently, due to the need for increased efficiency and high standards of animal welfare, the Fair family took the decision to create a new dairy unit on a Greenfield site to replace traditional buildings which were no longer considered suitable for modern milk production. Buildings at Brookside and Yew Tree, two of the three original farms, have already been developed into residential dwellings. The new farm at Poulton can house 600 cows plus 300 young stock on sand bedded cubicles. Yards and passageways are cleaned by a floodwash system. The cows are milked in a 60 point rotary parlour which can be done by two members of staff.

View of the 60 point rotary parlour.

Cows housed on sand bedded cubicles.

Self-loading mixing and feeding wagon at the silage clamp face.

Over the last sixty or so years, the farming industry has changed dramatically. The size of the dairy herd has risen considerably in recent years as smaller farms, no longer financially viable, have been absorbed into larger units which benefit from the economies of scale. Modern dairy units enable large cow numbers to be managed by relatively few staff as the number of people wanting to work in the industry has declined.

Farm machinery has also grown in size, variety, technology and cost. On many farms contractors are employed to carry out field work such as ploughing, manure spreading and crop harvesting. They have large state-of-the-art equipment which covers the ground in record time and experienced workers familiar with the machinery. It is difficult to justify capital expenditure on machinery for seasonal use on all but the largest farms.

Other changes in the farming industry over the last few years have shown a greater awareness of the need to balance the increase in productivity against the welfare of wildlife. As a predominantly dairy farming area we have retained the field hedges but farmers have been encouraged to leave a margin around their crops to maintain the wildlife habitat. Robert Bradshaw who lived at The Acres, Pulford, until the 1970s is renowned for his hedgecutting skills and keeping the parish looking neat and tidy.

In this parish in 2010 only 3 dairy farms remain:- New Brookside Farm, Poulton, Park Farm, Poulton and Oldfields Farm, Cuckoo's Nest. As the world population grows, food security becomes an ever more important issue, and hopefully the farmers in the Parish of Poulton and Pulford will continue to make their contribution to the well-being and prosperity of the UK.

Acknowledgements.

The author would like to thank the following who have kindly provided information and advice in the preparation of this chapter:

George Ashworth
Robert Bradshaw
Geoff Charlsworth
Geoff Edge
Gerry & Margaret Fair
Richard Fair
Stan Fish
Vera Gillam
Harold Gordon
Derek & Jill Gosmore
Doug Haynes
Diana Houlbrooke
Ms Louise Martin, archivist, Eaton Estates
Carol Moore
Edna, Lady Wilson

Parish Church of St Mary the Virgin

By Michael Nethercott

Pulford Church, a distinctive local landmark, visible on a clear day from the top of Moel Famau, and the 'bus stop' for Chester, Wrexham and lately, Barmouth, is the enduring place of worship for the local Christian community. A church has existed on this site for many centuries with a succession of church buildings. The Parish of St Mary the Virgin, Pulford, with its Rectory, was flourishing at the turn of the 19th century, when larger families existed than today's, necessitating not only a parish church but also a school, the Pulford Church of England School. At this time, a large choir consisting mainly of Pulford schoolboys provided tuneful accompaniment to the religious services for the faithful. One has to remember that during this period, transport for most people was limited to the pony and trap, or the occasional bicycle, otherwise all local journeys would have been on foot or horseback. Maybe that was one of the reasons a small chapel was established in a disused school on the Straight Mile at Poulton, which was known as St Chad's Mission Room,[1] with Sunday services conducted by the then Rector of Pulford, the Reverend Harry Branscombe (Rector from 1900 to 1905).

In her recollections the late Madge Kelly, a local resident, who was born in the 'Black & Whites' in a remote part of Poulton, took pride in the fact that from the age of five she walked every day to Pulford School and to Pulford Church every Sunday; a daily distance of more than two miles. She lived to the age of 96 years.

The earliest recorded Christian foundation within our present day parish occurred at Poulton in the middle of the twelfth century and is described in more detail in Chapter 1. At around the time this Cistercian foundation moved to Dieulacres in Staffordshire c 1214, a certain Hugo is recorded as the first Rector of Pulford, and so from the

Ladies in their 'Sunday Best' leaving Church Bank circa 1907

reign of King Richard I, worship in this village has been led by a succession of rectors believed to be unbroken to the present day, and since 1551 their work has been recorded in a fine set of church books.

In later times the church authorities exercised powers over their local communities. The following entry was found in the Pulford Town Book of 1801[2] to address the poor condition of the church and decide on levying a tax on the local population to cover the costs of regular maintenance:

> *"Meeting ... held at the house of Mr Leigh of Pulford in consequence of the very indecent state to which the church had suffered ...... it was unanimously agreed that the following solutions should be put into execution at times therein specified viz we, the Minister & Church Wardens & other parishioners of the Parish of Pulford in the County &*

Diocese of Chester, names therein subscribed do hereby this 16th day of October 1801, at our Vestry Meeting appointed for that purpose, agree on the part of ourselves individually, who have here subscribed, to board the flooring of all seats in the Parish Church of Pulford on or before 24 December 1801 & also we agree & find ourselves that we will on or before 16 November 1801 regulate the seats as agreed on, & now perfectly understood by each of us without any mental reservation - & also promise a pulpit cushion of the quality now agreed upon on or before the said 16th November 1801 - & also that the Pulpit shall be waxed & beautified & the windows should & shall for the future be cleaned by the church as often as shall be deemed required by the officiating minister - & we being the majority of the Parish do now by those present agree & rate & tax all & every (one) of the inhabitants & parishioners of the above Parish."

[3] *A sketch by John Townshend c.1811 of Pulford Church Tower, seen from behind the smithy cottage close to Pulford Brook.*

The church building depicted in John Townshend's sketch survived until 1833.

The following description of this church can be found in "Notes on Churches" by the late Sir Stephen Glynne[4].

"The original church pulled down in 1834 was a small structure of late & poor rectilinear work which abounds in Cheshire, and consisted of a nave and chancel with a western tower which was embattled, and had a band of flowers and animals. The west doorway had a contracted arch, in the label figures of birds and beasts, and above a three lighted window of ordinary character set between two small niches. The windows of the body were square headed, and between the nave and the chancel a coarse wood screen. The font a plain octagon."

'By divine permission of the Lord Bishop of Chester' the building was taken down in 1833-34 and a new church built on the site. This new church was opened at a Service of Consecration on 9th December 1834. During the period of this rebuilding, permission was granted for divine service to be performed " in the Girls School …. situate near Poulton"[5]. Sir Stephen Glynne described the new 1834 church built by Lord Westminster as *"a cruciform, of red sandstone with an ugly western tower having graduated buttresses, and to which it is to be lamented that the former has given place. The style is late gothic, but not very happy."* This church had north and south transepts as well as the main nave that seated adult members of the congregation. Seating for children was provided on a balcony. The church deteriorated over the years with leaking roof, rickety pews and unsafe floor, necessitating its replacement. It was closed in 1881 to make way for the present church built on the very same site.

The building of the present church was begun in 1881 at the instigation of the first Duke of Westminster, Hugh Lupus, and was the gift of the Duke to the people of the parish. It was designed by Chester Architect, John Douglas, in the early decorated style, and built of red sandstone interlaced with lighter courses giving a pleasing decorative effect; consisting of chancel, nave, transepts, and a north-west tower with shingled spire, containing a clock and six bells; two more bells were added later. It was opened on New

Year's Day 1884 with due pomp and ceremony attended by the Duke and presided over by the Rt Reverend Bishop Kelly, Archdeacon of Macclesfield.

There are many interesting features both on the inside and the outside of the church, making it unmistakably 'Douglas' including fine stone carvings seldom observed by the visitor. The heavy roof timbers give a warmth to the interior. Behind the altar is a delicate monochrome triptych of very fine quality framed in carved oak.

The altar set for Holy Communion with red frontal to commemorate 'martyrs' and the Reredos in monochrome triptych form depicting The Nativity (centre) with the Adoration of the Magi and The Visitation of the Shepherds in the side panels

The south transept accommodates the vestry and the organ. At the rear of the nave is an unusual pillared font covered by a wrought iron grill of outstanding workmanship. But perhaps the finest feature is the stained glass, being of a very high standard, most of which was designed and executed by Heaton Butler and Bayne of London. The east window is very fine, being of five lights depicting scenes from the final stages of the Bible Story of Our Lord's life on earth. There is the Garden of Gethsemane, the Trial, the Crucifixion, the meeting at Emmaus and, finally, the Ascension. When the early morning sun's rays pour in through this window, the quality of the glass is shown at its best as it becomes a blaze of colour. A beautiful Kemp window depicting Faith, Love and Hope is seen on the north wall of the nave dedicated to the Reverend James Reynold Williams, Rector of Pulford from 1870 to 1900.

The present church, seen from Dodleston Lane, with the original finely pointed spire, as illustrated
in this 'tinted' post card c. 1912.
Note: the wooden shingles of the spire and pinnacles have been coloured the same as the roof tiles!
(Courtesy of Gaenor Chaloner)

The flourishing choir c. 1900

It may come as a surprise to some to read that electricity did not find its way into the church until 1953. A faculty was granted in February of that year to take down the paraffin lamps in the church, which were to be retained for possible emergency use, and to install electricity.[6] Brackets that held the lamps are still retained on the walls at the entrance to the Chancel.

The parish of Pulford ceased to be an independent unit in 1973 when pastoral reorganisation linked Pulford with Eccleston to form a single parish. Henceforth, the parish has served the two communities and provided opportunities for joint worship and sharing in social and recreational events.

On Wednesday 31 July 1991, in the early afternoon a fire started in the spire. Local people were horrified at the frightening spectacle of the church spire being engulfed in flame, thought to have been caused by an electrical fault. One can imagine the observer of this sad event feeling

The spire remains (courtesy of Martin Rigby)

the heat from the flames radiating in their face. The wooden structure and oak shingles were highly combustible and despite fire fighters tackling the blaze, the spire was totally destroyed. After almost a month's work of clearing the debris and constructing a temporary roof covering over the tower, the church was declared safe and services were able to be resumed almost uninterrupted while a new spire was being constructed. This was completed in 1993.

The Ringing Chamber of the tower fortunately escaped serious damage. The Commemorative Peal Boards mounted on the walls of the chamber from the late 1800s and the set of handbells stored in the chamber all survived unscathed. Today, a recently formed team of handbell ringers under the direction of Kate Fairhurst can be heard playing in church and elsewhere on special occasions.

The tower made safe after removal of the spire remains. Services were able to resume quickly in the church (courtesy of Martin Rigby)

Spire reconstruction   *The restored spire.*

The new spire was consecrated by the Archdeacon of Chester, the Venerable Geoffrey Turner at a service on the 2nd of May 1993 (courtesy of Martin Rigby)

The Handbell Ringers c. 1900 – the very same bells in use today!

The church bells were removed after the fire and returned for cleaning to John Taylor Bell Founders of Loughborough who cast the bells originally. They were re-hung and dedicated at a later date after the Spire consecration.

The church centenary

The church celebrated its centenary in 1984 with an exhibition and flower display during the weekend of 14th & 15th July.

The Rev. Hugh Linn, Rector from 1982 to 1998, recalled during the celebrations, how times have changed in Pulford Church through the ages:

"Quite the opposite of the 17th century Puritans was Rev. R.G. Lowndes (Rector 1911-52). He was an uncompromising Anglo-catholic, complete with smells and bells. His views were not shared by parishioners and, although the congregation dwindled, he kept up a full round of services which he recorded methodically, noting sermons on the Rosary, Devotion to the Sacred Heart, Confession and Hail Mary. On major festivals a Solemn High Mass was celebrated. (Incidentally it is not true, as is usually thought, that the church in Pulford suddenly "went high" in Fr. Lowndes' time: H.S. Branscombe (1900-1905) introduced a Daily Eucharist in 1901 and held Stations of the Cross on Good Friday. He patriotically celebrated a Requiem for Queen Victoria). Church life in Pulford has seen great changes over centuries. For all the changes the Church in Pulford continues as a testimony to the worship of Almighty God and the abiding truth of the Christian Faith."

Stained glass windows by Heaton, Butler & Bayne

The East Window depicting, L to R, the Garden of Gethsemane, the Trial, the Crucifixion, the shared meal at Emmaus & the Ascension

Window to the south of the Altar depicting the scene in Simon the Pharisee's house where a woman is washing Christ's feet with her tears

The Pillared Font

On the walls as you enter the Chancel are redundant paraffin lamp holders of the 'pre-electric days'

Stone carvings around the church

Either side of the Chancel north window

Either side of the East Window

Either side of the North Transept Window

Either side of the West Window

 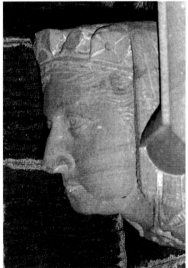

The heads of the First Duke of Westminster to the left and Queen Victoria right greet you on entering the church through the inner door of the porch.

THE PARISH OF
ECCLESTON & PULFORD

The service booklet used for the Queen's Silver Jubilee.

"Form of Prayer & of Thanksgiving to Almighty God on the Occasion of The Silver Jubilee of the Accession of Our Sovereign Lady Queen Elizabeth The Second".

This service was published with the approval of the Archbishops of Canterbury & York, the Cardinal Archbishop of Westminster and the Moderator of the Free Church Federal Council.

Pulford Church has hosted Civic Services. Here the Order of Service records the Civic Service for the Rural District Council in July 1965.

RURAL DISTRICT OF CHESTER

Chairman of the Council
COUNCILLOR Mrs. F. FAIR. J.P.

CIVIC SERVICE

Saint Mary the Virgin
Pulford

Sunday, 4th July, 1965
at 10.45 a.m.

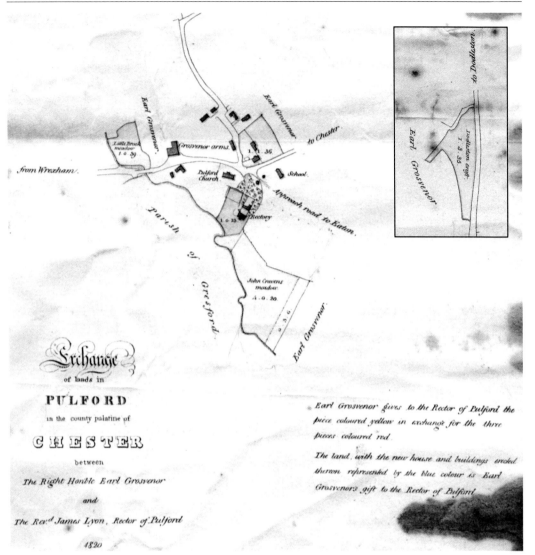

Reproduced by kind permission of the Revd. I. M. Thomas, Rector of Eccleston & Pulford Parish

[7] This map above of 1820 recording the exchange of land between the Earl Grosvenor and the Rector of Pulford shows interesting features then existing. Of particular interest is the old school on the same site as the subsequent school building, the Grosvenor Arms inn and opposite the Grosvenor Arms can be seen the small building of the smithy and next door two adjoined cottages. The exchange included land along Dodleston Lane shown inset. Opposite the Approach Road to Eaton two buildings, believed to be cottages are close to the site of the present Village Hall.

The Rectory, surviving to the present day after several alterations, is one of the oldest buildings in Pulford.

*Church Warden, the late Francis Glew, planting
the first tree of the new Millennium assisted by
the Rector, Rev. Jonathan Lumby and overseen
by Master James Hughes.
Reproduced by kind permission of Margaret Glew*

*The clock maker, J.B.Joyce Co. of
Whitchurch*

*A commemoration to the Rev.
J.R.Williams*

*Concerts feature in the church – seen here is the Rhos
Orpheus Male Choir in May 2009*

Rev. Jonathan Lumby's last service in Pulford Church on the 7th May 2005 with members of the congregation wishing him a long and happy retirement

The Salvation Army Band and the Rossett & District Royal British Legion leading the parade on a Battle of Britain Sunday in the 1970s. Grange Farm buildings, now converted to hotel accommodation, are seen to the right of the Grosvenor Arms. (courtesy of Audrey Gibson)

The church in Pulford is not only a place of worship, it is a symbol of our heritage, a natural focus in the community and a place of architectural beauty. Its continuing service to the life of the village is, as always, down to the support of its parishioners.

References:

1   Cheshire Record Office (CRO) reference P101/16
2   CRO reference MF 141
3   CRO reference D7007/1
4   "Notes on Churches" by the late Sir Stephen Glynne, Chetham Society, 2nd series, vol.32, 1884, reproduced by kind permission of the Council of the Chetham Society.
5   CRO reference P101/8
6   CRO reference P101/8/10
7   CRO reference P101/10/5

General reference has been made to the following:

Eccleston & Pulford Parish News – various editions
Ormerod – '*The History of the County Palatine & City of Chester*'.
The History of the Parish Church of St Mary the Virgin Pulford – Pulford & Poulton Local History Group.

Acknowledgements.

The author would like to thank especially the following who have kindly assisted in a variety of ways with the preparation of this chapter –

Cheshire Record Office, Gaenor Chaloner, the Reverend Hugh Linn, the Reverend Ian Thomas and Church Wardens: Michael Gledhill and Tom Walker.

Pulford Schools

The Early Schools of Pulford

By Gaenor Chaloner

It has proved extremely difficult to pinpoint the actual date when the first school was built in Pulford. The school records that have been saved only go back as far as 1813. However, the school does appear on a map/plan of Pulford in 1774 and from this evidence the school was obviously built before 1774 by the Warburton family of Arley Hall who owned the manor of Pulford prior to this date. There is an entry in the parish records of a baptism in 1773 which states, 'December 12th 1773 William son of John and Jane Humphreys of Pulford, Schoolmaster'. Presuming that he was a schoolmaster of Pulford School, this also points to a date for the establishing of the school as being prior to 1773.

*Map of Pulford
dated 1774*

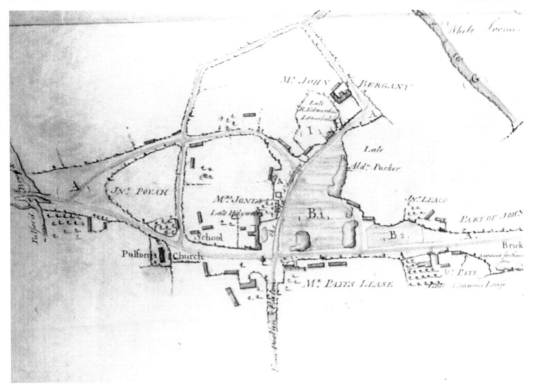

The school from the beginning was a Church of England school which at first consisted of separate buildings for boys' and girls' classes as the teaching of mixed classes was not an option for the teachers at this time. These buildings were situated on the Chester side of the corner of Dodleston Lane as the above map shows. The heating was by open coal fires and, according to the log books, the supply of coal often ran short and this must have made attending school quite miserable at times, especially during the winter months with poor fires. Owing to the lack of schools in the surrounding area, the catchment area for Pulford was a large one and appears to have not only taken pupils from Pulford and Poulton, but also Lavister, Trevallyn, Rossett and Gresford. Children had to pay not only to attend school but also for exercise and copy books and although it was referred to in the log books as 'school pence', it must have proved to be an added hardship for families, especially those with several children. For children who attended from outside the parish boundaries the cost was higher. The running of the school was overseen by several managers to whom the teaching staff were accountable. These managers were the equivalent of school Governors of today and the rules by which the school was run were those which were issued by the Lord of the Manor.

In 1867 there was a Reform Bill which was the first reference to a national system of elementary education which would be free and made school attendance compulsory. Although this does not appear to have been taken up in Pulford until 1870 when the First Education Act was passed which made attendance at school until the age of 13 compulsory. Although the above two Education Acts were implemented by the government it did not make any difference to the fact that in Pulford the schoolchildren had to continue to pay for their education until 1st September 1891 when the managers decided to accept the fee grant from the Education Department '*to free scholars from payment of the school pence*'.

The church played a large part in the children's education as the Rector took a very active roll in their education with lessons and examinations on the Holy Scriptures and the Catechism. They were also expected to attend the many church services which were held at that time, not just on Sundays but also midweek services. There was an expectation that they also attend from time to time services which were held at the cathedral. The school was part of the Chester Sunday School Union which meant that pupils had to attend Sunday school and sit exams on religion. Pupils had many lessons in the scriptures which were taken by the Rector of Pulford. Records show also that one of the managers in the 1870s, Mr. Massie, took lessons twice a week in the collect and gospel.

The cleaning of the school was part of school life for the children and monitors were set the task of 'brushing up' the classrooms after lessons. The decoration of the parish church for Christmas was part of school duties as the boys were sent out into the woods to collect ivy, holly and other greenery whilst the girls, during their sewing classes, spent their time sewing the leaves together to make the decorations.

Absenteeism was an ongoing problem. Sickness was rife amongst the children caused by illnesses such as smallpox, chin cough (whooping cough), measles, scarlet fever - to mention just a few; these illnesses were a constant threat to the children's wellbeing. Illness was not the only reason for absenteeism as children were expected to do their fair share of work at home by helping in the house and outdoor work especially when it was time to set or lift potatoes and the gathering of fruits such as blackberries etc. At times when absenteeism became a major problem, the rules which were set out by the Lord of the Manor were issued to all the families and appear to have made a difference for a while.

The log books which were kept by the headmaster are a wonderful insight not only into school life but also into village life, as there are many references to extreme weather conditions and the various activities which went on in the village. Some examples taken from the log books are as follows:

March 1872
"The issuing of Lord Westminster's pamphlets on rules has had the desired effect so far for very seldom anyone is absent without leave".

June 1872
"Tuesday in the afternoon of this week we had one of the most tremendous thunderstorms on record. In fact old men said they had never heard or seen it so terrific. The lightening and thunder was awfully grand. The hail stones were nearly as large as pigeon eggs. Never known such a storm before".

November 1872
"Wednesday of this week was the scene of a tremendous storm of wind, it blew in perfect hurricanes leaving trees up, blowing chimneys down, blowing stacks away and scattering chimney pots and slates in all directions".

March 1877
"Just allowed the children to go to the front to watch the cavalry go by for a few minutes".

One of the most interesting items in the log books was a reference to the experimental teaching of mixed sex classes. Mr. Clarke, the headmaster at the time, tried out mixed education and found it to be extremely useful and beneficial to the children's education but unfortunately the managers disagreed with his efforts as he reports in his log.

"I do not think that the managers have been wise in giving such a short a trial to the mixed school arrangement. The children as a whole were getting a better education last year than they are now".

Mr. Clarke left the school soon afterwards; could it have been because of his disillusionment with the managers in their failure to support his forward-thinking method of teaching?

The pupils were given an annual treat by the Marquess of Westminster which included play followed by a tea and was usually held on the Rectory lawn. The Marquess and his family attended and on occasions the villagers were also invited. Mr. Massie, who was one of the school managers, also gave the children an annual treat which took place either at the 'Park' at Pulford Hall or at Iron Bridge. One such occasion in 1875 which unfortunately did not turn out as expected was reported in the log books:

> *"Mr. Massie's "Iron Bridge" tea party. A holiday was given in the afternoon and we all repaired to the Iron Bridge. Taking our eatables- intending as usual to get the tea at Mr. Manley's who is the keeper of the said bridge. But fancy our disappointment when we got there we were told that they could not do with us that day in consequence of having a large party from Chester (who had previously arranged with Mr. Manley to provide for). Well there was no help for it- so we all looked at each other very perplexed and we had to retrace our steps to Pulford and have it in school the following day."*

For the children, some of whom would be quite young, it must have proved to be an extremely tiring event, having to make such a long walk down the drives to Iron Bridge and back.

An extra half day or a whole day were also given as holidays on occasions such as the day in February 1874 when *"our most noble Marquis having the title of Duke conferred upon him."* Also a holiday was given when Lord Grosvenor came of age and any other occasion within the family such as marriages. Every Shrove Tuesday the school closed for a half-day holiday.

The game of cricket was introduced to the school by the Head Master, Joseph Draper, in 1876 and in the 1800s geography was substituted for history. The earliest record of school photographs being taken was in 1880. This photograph was taken by Mr. Green of Chester but unfortunately a copy of this particular one has eluded us. However, there are several early photographs that did survive.

Class photograph 1891

Class photograph 1894

The precise date for the new school being built on a site across the road from the old one has yet to be found but it did partially move across the road at some point before 1822 and in 1877 it was written that *"one of the managers came and spoke about matters concerning the new building"*. This in fact was referring to the alterations and enlargements of the school building which took place in 1879 under the instructions of the architect, John Douglas.

On the 3rd March 1903 notice was received from the Board of Education that from April 1st the official number of the school is 240.

*The new School
Building*

References.

The Grosvenor Family Archive Box F/Bundle 7/27 reproduced by Cheshire Record Office.

Cheshire Record Office; MF283/128, SL 112/1/2 and MF 141

Pulford School post 1900

By Marian Davies

From the year 1900 Mr. Leonard Bebbington was now Head Teacher and living in School House. During his time as head teacher until his successor took over in 1919, he would have seen the school through the war period at a time when the trauma of war would have been very unsettling for the pupils, some of whom would have seen their older relatives called up to the front lines.

The 1902 Education Act saw Church Schools passing under the jurisdiction of their respective Education Authority, so from 1st July 1903 Pulford began to operate under the Cheshire Local Education Authority.

Miss Wright took the Middle class (she later became Head Teacher at Dodleston) and
Mrs. Williams the Infant class. Gardening seemed to be very popular as the photograph shows.

During Mr Bebbington's time, the children and teachers received a special treat at the invitation of the Duke of Westminster to attend a Christmas Party at Eaton Hall.

Older pupils with Mr Bebbington, Head Teacher in 1919, just before his retirement

Mr. Ackerley was appointed Head Teacher in 1919, but there is very little in the school records through the 1920s and 1930s. The 12th May, 1937 was the occasion of the Coronation of King George VI and Queen Elizabeth, and all pupils were presented with a souvenir copy of The New Testament (below). Miss Benbow and Mrs Williams were on the staff at the time, which was to change with the outbreak of the Second World War in 1939. Mrs. Ackerley took over the middle class and pupil numbers changed week by week as children were evacuated to the country from Liverpool and Merseyside.

Mr Bebbington taking the boys in 'kitchen gardening' c.1919 to encourage the growing of vegetables at a time when food would have been in short supply after the war

In the early 1940s school meals were introduced. These came from a central kitchen in the Chester area and were served to the children in a wooden building called 'The Café' which was located by the local shop. It was not until the 1950s that a new canteen was built on the school drive.

The Duke of Westminster continued to send Christmas presents for all the children in school up to about 1941 when the Duke's family moved away from Eaton Hall.

Mr. Ackerley died in the mid-forties and was succeeded as Head Teacher by his wife Mrs. Ackerley. During the Second World War an air raid shelter was built on the drive to the school and pupils had a small tin box inside the shelter which contained snacks and emergency rations so that, in the event of having to stay for a prolonged period during an air raid, the pupils and teachers would have sustenance.

In the 1944 Education Act the 'Eleven Plus' exam was introduced which was used to select pupils for Grammar School placement. The school leaving age went up from fourteen to fifteen in 1949. The older boys and girls went once a week by coach to a Chester school for woodwork and cookery.

In the nineteen-fifties the Head Teacher was Mr. Randles. An ex-pupil relates that school trips took place to various places of educational interest; one in particular was a visit to see the Royal Train with Her Majesty the Queen on board at the nearby Dodleston Crossing on the Great Western Railway. They waved their flags but the train seemed to go by very quickly.

Children from Rossett and Lavister were no longer admitted as a new school in Rossett was built (St. Peter's) and the Cheshire Education Authority would no longer allow pupils from Wales to attend Pulford School. In 1959 Secondary Education became available and children then travelled by coach to the newly opened Christleton Secondary Modern. In 1976 Dee High School was opened and children from this area attended there; the name of this school was later changed to Bishop's High School.

School group
c. 1946

In 1964 Mr. Randles moved to teach at Ellesmere Port and Mr. James Pritchard became the head teacher, followed some three years later by Mr. Glyn Pritchard, no relation. There were various additions to the school in the 1960s and 1970s, namely; a Police "Lollypop" lady; Mid-day Assistants on playground duty at lunch time; a part time Secretary and also the forming of a Parent Teacher Association. A weekly visit to the Christleton swimming baths for the older children was also introduced at this time.

The school celebrated its Centenary in 1970. A week of celebration took place with an outing to Conway on Saturday 11th July organised by the Parent Teacher Association. All children were presented with Bibles, and a Service of Thanksgiving was held on Sunday 12th July which was attended by The Duke and Duchess of Westminster.

The Duke & Duchess of Westminster are welcomed by the Rev. Coleman Harrison to the school centenary service of thanksgiving (Photo reproduced courtesy of the Chester Chronicle)

1975 was European Architectural Heritage Year and the City of Chester was one of four places selected in the United Kingdom to represent an aspect of outstanding heritage. Pulford, being one of the gateways to our ancient city, celebrated the occasion in July with a festival of flowers and an exhibition of Parish History in which the school took part.

During the mid-seventies a Pre-school Nursery Group was held in the school, that included Eccleston, Dodleston, Huntington and Pulford areas, and met one half-day each week.

School group c. 1971 with teacher Mrs Ruth Nuttall and head teacher Glyn Pritchard

In the late 1970s The Duke of Westminster started to invite all the children from the schools within the Eaton Estate to a firework display at Eaton Hall on 5th November, an event that continues to this day.

Courtesy of Cllr Jim Dryland

In May 1981 Her Grace the Duchess of Westminster celebrated her 21st Birthday by inviting all children from the schools on the Eaton Estate to a party at Eaton Hall with entertainment by Ken Dodd and the Diddy Men. His Grace also presented commemorative mugs to all pupils on the occasion of the wedding of Prince Charles and Lady Diana Spencer on the 29th July 1981.

By early 1981 pupil numbers were dropping and there were no signs of any increase in the future. Numbers were down to eighteen and closure seemed inevitable to give pupils more scope in their education. Various ideas were put forward to try to keep the school open, but it was on the 21st July 1982 when the school finally closed. A sad day for Pulford, but for the twelve children who were due to continue their primary education and join Eccleston School that September together with pupils from Aldford School, also closing at the same time, they would have new friends and more competition to look forward to.

The last eighteen pupils just before closure

The Reverend Laurie Skipper handing over the notice of closure to Head Teacher, Glyn Pritchard

Village Enterprise

Public Houses of Pulford

By Gaenor Chaloner

Alcohol has been consumed throughout history, not only for the reasons it is drunk today but out of sheer necessity as the water in earlier times was unfit for consumption, and the brewing process killed off waterborne diseases. Even before the Roman period in this country wine was being imported and of course ale was being brewed 'at home'. The later Middle Ages brought in coaching houses which provided food and shelter for the traveller as well as stabling for the weary horses.

Inns, or 'Public Houses', began to spring up nationwide during the 16th century when the brewing process was still a necessity. The task of brewing the ale fell to the woman of the household and was probably done as often as every other day. Somewhere along the line came the realisation that there was money to be made in the brewing and selling of ale and from 1552 annual licences were granted to households for the selling of ale and porter, porter being a dark ale akin to stout.

These early ale houses were exactly that, ordinary houses from which the occupier was granted a licence to sell ale. The earliest licence in Pulford was granted in 1636 to William Halliwell, followed by Richard Lloyd in 1768-70 and then Benjamin Bennion 1772-1775. This licence overlapped with an additional licence being granted to John Leigh in 1768. This situation of two licensed premises in Pulford lasted for only seven years; the licence that was to remain for all time was that of John Leigh and was to stay within his family for over a century. It is worth remembering that the whole of Pulford was a manor and that everyone living here were tenants of the Lord of Pulford who owned the manor. There were only two properties in Pulford that were privately owned and they were Meadow House Farm and Pulford Hall but the owners still paid chief rent to the Lord of the Manor. During the 1600s the population of Pulford was 130 with one Inn. 170 in the 1700s with two inns and in 1801 when reverting back to one inn the population was 275.

Conditions attached to the granting of a licence were as follows:

"Whereas the above bounden alehouse keepers are severally licensed to sell ale for one year from the twenty ninth day of this present month of September (1797) in the houses wherein they dwell. Now if they or any of them, their or any of their assigns or any other person or persons selling ale by the virtue of the above licences shall neglect to keep and maintain good order and rule or shall suffer any unlawful games to be used or disorders to be committed in his or her dwelling house or houses or any outhouse yard, alehouse keepers and their representatives sureties shall be void and of non effect."

The first purpose-built public house in Pulford had a dual roll of both public house and a working farm and was given the name of "The Talbot" which was built between 1774 and 1788 as it does not appear on a map of 1774, but there is a reference to a song being sung at the Talbot at Lord Belgrave's coming of age in 1788.

In 1814 the ownership of the Manor of Pulford changes and is now transferred to Earl Grosvenor which included the Talbot. Soon after the purchase the name was changed from the Talbot to the Grosvenor Arms, the name of which appears on a map/plan of Pulford of 1822. The Tithe map of 1837 for Pulford describes the inn as "Public House and garden, farmhouse buildings, yard and garden with nine fields which were used for a mixture of wheat, oats, clover, arable, hay and pasture". By 1850 the Grosvenor was also a post office receiving house and continues under the Leigh family's reign as publican/farmers in Pulford until 1873 with the deaths of first Timothy Leigh and then his widow, Ann.

These inns generally became the victims of their own success as more and more men were drinking which in turn had a detrimental effect on both village and home life. This became a major problem because it led directly to the springing up of 'Men's Reading Rooms' in villages to try and combat this trend and all the problems associated with it. These rooms were originally for men only and were meant as an alternative to the way of life that had developed. The one which was built here in Pulford is now the Village Hall. On the other hand, although this problem had become really serious, it should also be mentioned that the Inn in Pulford was often used for the good of the village, such as meetings of the church council (*these church meetings are recorded in the parish records as being held at the house of Mr. Leigh*) and providing teas after the parades of the Oddfellows, to mention but two of the many other occasions which were celebrated there.

In 1891 the Inn was described as a free house; two beds for travellers and accommodation for supplying 50 persons with refreshments plus one stable and four stalls.

In 1897 the building underwent major alterations under the direction of architect John Douglas. The building work was carried out by the Parker Brothers at a cost of £1,680.0.0.

The Grosvenor Arms c.1932

When the village of Pulford was sold off by the Duke of Westminster in 1919 the Grosvenor Arms along with the farmland was bought by William Dyke on the 15th May. The total acreage at the time of sale was 60.458.

The Dyke family had farmed in Pulford for many years at Brookside Farm before and after the building of the new farmhouse. William Dyke married Martha Dutton of Tarvin and although they had several children who lived to adulthood, there were other children that did not survive infancy. Although the loss of children at that time and earlier was a common occurrence, it must have been heartbreaking for the families to lose children at such young ages. The Dyke family were no exception to this as the children they lost were George aged 1 month in 1897, Edith aged 11 months in 1899, Frank aged 4 days in 1899, Pattie aged 11 hours in 1900 and Ethel Rose aged 11 months in 1903.

The Dyke family

1919 saw the celebrations which were held at the Grosvenor for a homecoming dinner for the men of the village who had managed to survive the ravages of the First World War. It was obviously quite an occasion in the village as is shown by the menu illustrated below.

The Menu for the Home Coming dinner for the Troops of Pulford

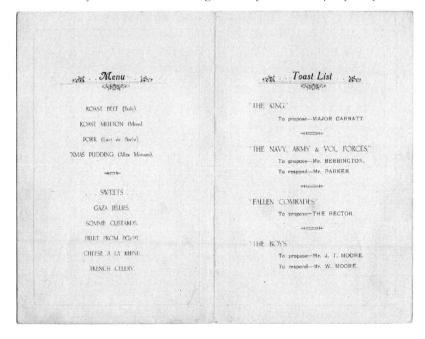

*The Grosvenor
Bowling Team*

During William Dyke's time as landlord of the Grosvenor Arms a bowling green was formed in the garden area and a thriving bowling club was started which was well attended by the men of the village.

1	2	3	4	5	6	7	8	9	10	11
JIMMY PROBIN	TOM MOORE	ARTHUR FEARNALL	FRANK LLOYD	BILLY B ROOKES	SID FEARNALL	BILL DYKE	TOM FAIR	BILL DAVIES	WILLIAM DYKE	JACK DYKE
1	2		3	4		5		6		7
HARRY GROOME		MATHEWS	WILL MOORE	JOHNSON		JIM MORGAN		MR HUMPHREYS		MR POWELL

In 1932 William Dyke decided to separate the farmland from the hotel and sold the Grosvenor Arms plus 5,014 square yards of land to Albert Sherriff. An auction for the sale was held at the Blossoms Hotel, Chester, on Thursday, September 29th 1932 at 3 o'clock.

The description of the building as described in the auction brochure is as follows:

"Spacious entrance hall and well fitted bar.
Large billiard room
Smoke room or dining room
Tap room to the rear of the bar with separate entrance from the hotel yard
Gentlemen's lavatory, basin and w.c.

Good kitchen
Back kitchen and pantry with back hall and entrance from
the yard
On first floor
Drawing room
Five large bedrooms
Commodious club room
Bathroom with bath, lavatory, basin and w.c.
Second floor
Six bedrooms
Tank room
Underneath the main portion of the building are;
The large dry, well ventilated and lighted cellars
Outside offices comprise;
Laundry room
Closed motor shed adaptable for a garage
Two store houses
Closed motor shed with rooms over
Urinal and large yard.
On each side of the premises are gardens and orchard; the other
laid out as a lawn with sunk dancing plot or bowling green."

(note there is no mention of a ladies w.c., obviously Public
Houses were still a male bastion.)

*The Grosvenor
Pulford Hotel as
seen today*

This sale was followed ten years later by the sale of the farmland to Dudley Beck of Quaintways Ltd. 1946 brings yet another sale, this time Minnie Sherriff (Albert's widow) sold the hotel to Chester Northgate Brewery which brought in an endless stream of managers. The hotel is now owned by Harold and Sue Nelson who have totally transformed it into a very large and thriving hotel of quality as can be seen today and it is now renamed 'The Grosvenor Pulford Hotel'.

The farm land also changed hands; in 1954 it was bought by Mr. and Mrs. Don Wilson who had a new farmhouse built and the farm was then renamed The Grange. Mr. and Mrs Tom Dodd became the last owners of the Grange, which ceased as a working farm on the 1st October 1982.

References

The Alehouse and Alehouse keepers of Cheshire 1629-1829. A.J. Macgregor

Cheshire Record Office QDV 2, Land Tax Assessments

Bagshaw's Cheshire Trade Directory

White's Trade Directory

Morris and Co. Directory

Slater's Directory

Kelly's Directory

Cheshire Record Office QPCa 6 Chester Petty Session, Register of Victuallers

Cheshire Record Office QDL 2/1/5 Vituallers Recognizances 1797

Census for Pulford 1841-1901

Cheshire Record Office MF 141, Pulford Parish Records

Auction Brochure of sale in 1932

The History of the Village Shop and Post Office

By Gaenor Chaloner

At the edge of Pulford on the border between England and Wales, opposite what is now the Grosvenor Pulford Hotel, stood a smithy and two cottages on the bank of Pulford Brook. In the late 1700s the Blacksmith was James Dean who leased the Smithy until 1806 when both James and his wife died during the month of April. The Smithy was then taken over by their son, also James, and in the list for Land Taxes, the Smithy was registered as James Dean and Company. James unfortunately died at the age of 48 in 1824 which left his widow to run the business, employing Blacksmith Jonathon Hopley who lived with his family in the second cottage on the site. Mary Dean died in 1853 leaving Jonathon Hopley the opportunity to apply for the tenancy himself.

The site on which the Smithy once stood

By the census for 1861, Jonathon Hopley is not only a blacksmith but he was also running a grocer's shop in which his daughter Mary was later to serve as a shop assistant. Evidence found so far points to the smithy being the first shop in the village. At a later date it was also to become the local Post Office. It certainly must have made a great difference to the local people not only to have a shop in the village but also their own Post office.

Jonathon Hopley died in 1881 and his wife Martha died the following year. After their deaths it appears that both of the children left the village. It was about this time that the village was being rebuilt by the Duke of Westminster. One of the many farms that were to have a new farmhouse was Brookside which was built in 1885 and when the Dyke family moved into the new farmhouse, the old one became known as the Pump Cottages.

The "new" Brookside Farmhouse

It was decided that the now empty farmhouse was to become the new post office and shop which was run by a young man named Walter Thomas who was also a joiner by trade, which probably meant that his wife actually ran the shop. The old smithy plus the two cottages were demolished making room for the widening of the main Wrexham to Chester road.

Artist's impression of the old Post Office c. 1900 (Watercolour: Michael Nethercott)

Soon after 1901 the lease of the shop was taken over by Mrs. Allen, but only for a short period of time.

A later view of the shop and Post Office c.1970)

In 1919 when the Duke of Westminster sold the manor of Pulford, the shop was bought by Mrs. Elizabeth Brooks (neé Moore). On her retirement, the shop was let to Mrs. Waterer until 1951 when it was taken over by Mr. and Mrs. S. N. Roberts. It continued as a thriving business which also became the heart and soul of the community, where the villagers doing their shopping were able to keep in touch with each other on what was happening in the village. Mr. and Mrs. Roberts had a new purpose-built shop erected in 1977 close to the site of the old one which in turn reverted back into a dwelling. In 1981 the shop was sold to Mr. Berry who after a short period of time sold it on to Mr. and Mrs. Gittings.

A photograph of the new purpose-built shop

July 1999 brought the devastating news that the shop was to close its doors and, although various attempts were made by villagers to try and prevent its closure, it did finally close.

The closure left the village with a great void as it meant local people no longer had the convenience of being able to shop in their own village but, more importantly, they no longer had the opportunity to meet with the other members of the community on a daily basis. Unfortunately, it took the heart out of the community spirit in the village which we had enjoyed for so many years and sadly it is something that the village will never be able to recapture.

The closure of the shop with local councillors and members of the public showing their disapproval.
(photo published courtesy of the Chester Chronicle)

References

Census for Pulford and Poulton 1841-1901
Cheshire Record Office MF 141, Parish records

Pulford Garage

By Michael Nethercott

*Photograph
of the early
1930s showing
Chevrolets. Note
the price of the
van at £225!
Courtesy of
Derek Moulton*

From the recollections of local residents it seems likely that the original garage, known as Brookes Brothers Garage, was in existence by 1926. In those days, the servicing and maintenance of motor vehicles would have demanded quite advanced skills of the time from the mechanics. As well as the garage, the brothers built a vehicle repair depot on the opposite side of Wrexham Road. From the photograph c. early 1930s one can observe the garage dealing in Chevrolet cars and vans. Joan Brookes, the daughter of Charlie, one of the brothers, would later marry to become Joan Roberts and together with her husband would run the village shop and post office.

Brookes Bros, Garage, Pulford Nr. Wrexham.

The garage for many years was both a petrol station and car servicing workshop. Wilf Stockton and Nancy Owen were well known employees.

The garage and repair depot were sold in 1956, the latter becoming Chaloner's Iron and Steel Merchants, now the site of Burganey and Ivy Courts. Mr & Mrs McCready took over the running of the garage which became Pulford Service Station selling Fina petrol.   The McCreadys demolished the garage in c 1962-3, building the present garage on the same site. Mrs McCready continued to run the garage after the death of her husband until it was sold to a Brain Jones in 1972 to become 'Brian Jones Performance Cars', when the petrol pumps were removed and the garage returned to car sales and servicing.

It was in 1978 that Mr Jones divided the garage into a workshop and antiques shop, the workshop being run by Derek Moulton. Some nine years later the antiques shop closed and Derek bought the garage, modernised it and extended the premises to what it is today, trading under the name 'D. M. Performance Cars', a well respected vehicle repair workshop and sales garage known throughout the surrounding area.

W. H. Chaloner & Son. Ltd

By Gaenor Chaloner

William Henry Chaloner and his family moved into Pulford in 1956 having bought Park House and the land associated with it; later he was also to buy Carden Cottage which was situated next door. The business he ran was that of 'Iron and Steel Merchant' which had been previously run from Lache Hall, near Chester.

Bringing a business of this nature into a small village, especially as it was situated in the centre, could have been the cause of unrest in the village. Quite the opposite was true. It was readily accepted by the villagers as the previous business that occupied the site was of a similar nature.

The family did their utmost to make the business as acceptable as possible to the village by undertaking various alterations to the property, with the purpose of keeping their operations shielded as much as possible from the village. Also every effort was made to keep all areas as neat and tidy as possible. This must have been quite a task as there was a constant stream of lorries in and out of the site not to mention the machinery which was necessary for the work.

The firm dealt in the main with John Summers Steel Works and Brymbo Steel works until their closure and also Liverpool Docks through which the metal was exported. They also traded with various other factories throughout the area.

In the early days before complete mechanisation, as in most trades, the work was extremely hard with long hours but all this helped to create a successful business. When William died, his sons took over the running of the business and carried it on in the same way as their father before them. When the sons were approaching retirement they decided to sell both of the houses with the land in 1995 to Bell Meadow for the development of a small housing estate. New premises were bought for the continuation of the business at Llay Industrial Estate, near Wrexham. The grandsons of William Henry Chaloner now run the business which continues to flourish.

Occupations in 1851

By Gaenor Chaloner

Taking a snapshot at the year 1851, we find in the census for Pulford and Poulton the following people and their occupations:

Pulford
John Cohen, School Master
Jane Woolley, School Mistress
Rev. J.R. Lyon, Rector
Mary Dean, Proprietress of the Smithy
Jonathon Hopley, Blacksmith
Richard Walker, Blacksmith
Sam Hughes, Butcher
William Hughes, Butcher
John Hughes, Butcher
Catherine Hill, Laundress
Mary Hill, Laundress
Richard Jones, House Painter
John Davis, House Painter
Joseph Jones, Shoemaker
Edward Williams, Shoemaker
Edward Jones, Joiner
William Morris, Carter
George Brough, Tilemaker
James Kirkham, Carpenter
Edward Jones, Engineer
James Kirkham, Inspector of Buildings
William Wildig, Station Master
James Morgan, Gamekeeper
John Richardson, Sawyer
Timothy Leigh, Innkeeper

Pulford Farmers

John Leigh

James Ley

Thomas Saldine

William Hughes

Jane Lowe

Samuel Moore

Joshua Gregory

James Wainwright

Poulton

Thomas Pate, Thatcher

Thomas Jones, Drainer

Charles Leech, Wheelwright

John Powell, Carter

Joseph Morris, Carpenter

Charles Thomas, Blacksmith

Farmers

Mary Williams

William Pickering

Robert Jones

Evan Evans

John Phillips

The Burganey Family of Pulford Hall

By Gaenor Chaloner and Dominic Byrne

Introduction;

The Lordship of the Manor of Pulford in the latter half of the 16th century was held by the Warburton family of Arley Hall and almost all of the village was in their possession. However, the Pulford family, whose ancestors had previously held the Lordship of this manor and who had taken the name of the village as their surname, still had some property here.

In the early 17th century Hugh Pulford sold some land and houses to Anthony Burganey. This gave the Burganey family a small foothold in the village, which would be their home for almost 250 years.

The Burganey Coat of Arms

Due to the scarcity of records, it is difficult to piece together the early history of the Burganey family before 1600. Although the information is somewhat fragmented, it is still intriguing and there are indications that the family were of French origin. The earliest records thus far located of the Burganey family are of two brothers, Thomas born in 1531 and John born two years later in 1533. The latter is probably the John Burgonyon alias or otherwise known as John Frenchman, a surgeon of Chester who was the subject of an inquisition for the then King and Queen (Philip and Mary). 'On the 1st July 1556 he broke into the house of Robert Dryhurst, merchant, of Bridge Street, Chester, and stole 28 pounds of "good and lawful money" from the purse of the said Robert Dryhurst.' The following year (1557) he was "indicted for stealing from a house, a cap case, a payre of gloves, and three veils, three bed cloths, value 30s". This John Burgonyon was reputedly the father of Anthony Burganey of Wootton Underwood, Buckinghamshire, and later of Holt, Denbighshire.

"Arms – Gules. A Tower Or. Crest – On a wreath – a Mount Vert – and thereon a like Tower." (description of the Burganey Coat of Arms by Randle Holme III)

A Richard Burganey is recorded as renting land in Dodleston in 1560. The Burganeys' of Dodleston and Pulford were related and shared similar Christian names which can be a cause of confusion.

The parish records in Pulford, although very sketchy for these early dates, contain the earliest evidence of the Burganey family living in Pulford. There are two early legible entries relating to the family; the first is the marriage of Thomas Burgenye on June 8th 1578 and the second is the baptism of John Burganey, son of Nicholas in 1608.

The above Anthony Burganey of Holt married Catherine Bostock of Churton. He is credited with the building of Pulford Hall circa 1609. We have been unable to find any evidence to substantiate this claim and unfortunately do not know on what it was originally based. However, it was Anthony who was responsible for establishing the rather spreadeagled estate and the family's greatly improved financial position. In the period 1606 to 1608 a number of transactions were recorded between Anthony Burganey and Hugh Pulford, concerning some houses and land in Pulford. In these property transactions he is always described as a "yeoman" of "Holte", while Hugh is usually referred to as "Hugh Pulford of Pulford, Co. Chester, gent". Anthony died in 1610. The following year an inventory of his assets records him as "of Lyons" which is the former name for Holt.

What has been established is that Anthony's son, William, who was born in Holt, did reside at Pulford Hall, and was married to a local girl Katherine Halliwell, a native of Pulford. The Halliwells' were a long-standing farming family in the district. Pulford, at this time, was a village with a very small population, the majority of whom were labourers or tenant farmers. It must have caused quite a stir to have the 'landed gentry' move into the village and build what must have been an imposing Hall. This residence would have been very 'grand' in comparison to the very modest thatched cottages which were the norm in the village for the period.

The Burganeys of Pulford had a very scattered estate some of which they owned and some which they held on long-term leases. They had property at Holt and Worthenbury in Denbighshire, Treuddyn, Leeswood and Hope in Flintshire and Dodleston and Pulford in Cheshire. They derived their income from leasing out this property.

William and Katherine had two children, a son baptised William who was born in 1620 and a daughter Joyce who was baptised in Pulford on 25th December 1636. The younger William enrolled in Corpus Christi College, Oxford, on 7th June 1637 and graduated with a B.A. on June 10th 1641. He appears to be the only Burganey listed in the Oxford University alumni. William married Elizabeth, daughter and co-heiress of David Lloyd of Hope parish.

The following is the Randle Holme III image of the combined Coat of Arms of the Burganey and Lloyd families. Randle records in his notes that it is carved on a tomb in Pulford churchyard. Unfortunately, this can no longer be found.

The Burganey Coat of Arms occupies the first and fourth quarters,
the second and third are those of the Lloyd family.

William and Elizabeth had four children. Their eldest, William, was born 1660. Their second child, Catherine, their only daughter was baptised on November 29th 1664. Anthony was born on 17th October 1665 but survived for just over one month and died 21st November. Their last born, Edward, born 30th October 1666, died the following day. This high infant mortality was the norm at the time, with approximately half the children dying before the age of five. With Elizabeth's death on 25th July 1670, William was left to care for his two young children alone. However, less than eight months later, on the 5th February 1671, he married Mary Pritchard, with whom he had two children, Mary born 1673 and Timothy born 1674.

Ormerod, in his History of Cheshire – 1882, quotes the following from a Latin manuscript written by William Burganey B.A. (i.e. Guliemus Burganaeus)

> *"About four miles from here lies Pulford, facing south in a pleasant and fertile location. Blessed with rich soil it marks the boundary of Chester's land against the Welsh. It is the village where I first crossed the threshold of existence; a gentle place which has given to my life the solace of retreat".*

The manuscript now reputedly in the archives of Yale University, was written and embellished with twenty one drawings, which included a view of Chester and a portrait of the author "Guliemus Burganaeus" of Pulford. It also contained a map of the world subscribed "per me T. Burgaynie". Our author and scholar passed away on August 25th 1689.

In 1689 his son William married Rachel, the daughter of Randle Holme III of Chester, and they had two children, William and Rachel. Sadly only four years into the marriage Rachel died on March 30th 1693 and was buried in St. Mary's, Chester. In 1695 William remarried, this time to Mary Vernon, daughter of William Vernon of Balderton with whom he had four children. They were baptised as follows: John March 17th 1696, Mary, Jan. 21st 1697; Catherine on Nov. 15th 1700 and the youngest Hannah 24th February 1706. Their father died on Dec. 23rd 1732 just short of his 70th birthday. The main beneficiary of his will, which was administered by his second wife, was his son John. For some reason not known to us, his two children, William and Rachel from his first marriage to Rachel Holme, seem to have been overlooked. However after his early death in 1707, their uncle, Randle Holme IV left Rachel £60 in his will. His own five children had all died young and predeceased him.

Rachel Holme was a member of the remarkable Holme family from Chester. Randle (Randulph) was the name given to four successive generations of the Holme family: Randle Holme I (1571-1655), Randle Holme II (1601 – 1659), Randle Holme III (1627 – 1700) and Randle Holme IV (1659 – 1707). The family played an important role in the municipal life of Chester, holding various positions such as mayor and sheriff at different periods. The family were avid collectors and left a manuscript collection of 261 volumes, an extremely important source of Cheshire's history. Rachel's father, Randle Holme III wrote and illustrated 'The Academy of Armory' (1688) which provides one of the most comprehensive glimpses we have for everyday life in 17th century England. All four were deeply involved in heraldry, and in the associated painting of memorial boards, many of which can still be seen in various churches in Cheshire. One of these memorial boards in memory of Rachel Holme and the Burganey family and attributed to Randle III, is on the south wall of the Parish Church of St. Mary's, Pulford. The fact that these boards were unsigned makes it difficult to know with certainty the identity of the original artist.

Pulford Memorial Board

(Photo reproduced by kind permission of Dr Andrew Gray)

*In the churchyard, under a faire stone lyeth
the bodyes of Will. Burgayny of Pulford son of
Anthony and of Katherine his wife*

-

*William Burganey of Pulford, Gen his son student
of Corpus Christi C'ollege in oxford died 25 Aug
1689; Elizabeth his wife dau. & coheire of David
Lloyd of ugh y monidd; in Hope died 25 July
1670: William his son Gen: married Rachell dau. to
Randle Holme of ye city; of Chester Gen. and had
issue William & Rachell. She died 30 March 1693
is buried in St. Mary's, in Chester.*

College of Arms Report March 2010

"During our research we were unable to find any record as to when the Burganey family received the right to bear arms. We consequently enlisted the aid of the College of Arms in London. After a thorough search they issued a report in March 2010 on which the following is based.

Between 1530 and 1687 the heralds visited each county to oversee the use of Arms and to record the pedigrees of the gentry. At each visitation the gentry, or those claiming to be gentry, were summoned before the heralds. Those who could provide no evidence of gentility or the right to bear Arms were compelled to sign a declaration disclaiming gentle status. The book "Pedigrees made at the Visitation of Cheshire 1613, ed. Sir George J. Armytage and J. Paul Rylands (Lancashire and Cheshire Record Society 58, 1909) contains a list based on B.L. Harleian Ms. 1070 f. 87 of those disclaiming gentle status at the 1613 visitation from Broxton hundred. Among the names is that of William Burganey of Pulford. Although the Harleian Ms. was not examined or its provenance determined "the entry strongly suggests that the Burganeys' could prove no right at the visitation of 1613".

The following is the Report's conclusion;
"Comprehensive searches in the official registers of Arms and pedigrees maintained by the College of Arms, including records of grants and confirmations, and of the heraldic visitations, have revealed no entries relating to the Burganey family of Pulford. The disclaimer above, taken with, the negative evidence from the official records, suggest that no right to Arms was possessed by this family. Randle Holme may have been acting beyond the law in painting a heraldic memorial for William Burganey; this board flattered the family that they were entitled to Arms."

In this context it is interesting to note that Randle Holme III had previously lost a court case to the Norroy King of Arms, Sir William Dugdale, who then proceeded to remove, deface or destroy many of Holme's illegal boards between 1667 and 1670.

William Burganey's only son from his second marriage to Mary Vernon, John Burganey, married Margaret Broughton of Gresford parish in Pulford church on 22nd April 1732. They had one son, born on the 10th Sept. 1736 and also baptised John. This boy's mother Margaret was buried on 18 April 1753 as was his father on 18th Dec. 1761.

John married Ann Pate, of Croes Howell in Gresford parish, with whom he had two children. Their only son John was baptised in Pulford church on March 26th 1775 and similarly their daughter Ann on Feb. 4th 1780. Their father died in 1788, and John aged just 13 was left as the sole surviving male of the Pulford branch of the Burganey family, and heir to Pulford Hall and their estates.

In March 1794 at the age of 19, John with the rank of Cornet was amongst the first batch of officers gazetted into the Ancient British Fencible Cavalry. This was a newly formed regiment which had been raised by Sir Watkin Williams Wynne of Wynstay Hall, Ruabon, in response to the alarming increase in the size of the French army in 1793. John, while serving as an officer with the regiment was also trying to run the estate at home. His mother kept him informed of estate matters and sought advice from him during his absence.

The regiment served in various locations on the British mainland until 1797 when they were ordered to sail for Ireland to help with the growing unrest there. This would later erupt as the 1798 Rebellion. John was rapidly promoted to Lieutenant, then Captain Lieutenant and finally Captain. In Ireland he served at first in the north of the country where the regiment gained a reputation for extreme brutality and was feared by the inhabitants.

On Easter Sunday 8th April 1798, following the imposition of martial law in County Wicklow in the east of the country, a troop of Ancient Britons led by Captain Burganey arrived in Newtownmountkennedy. Here they continued to mete out the same brutal treatment as they had done in the north. The worst atrocities occurred on the 11th April 1798 at the local fair. The events were witnessed by loyalist Thomas Parsons who recorded the events for his brother, Sir Lawrence Parsons M.P. and Commander of the King's Militia.

"Six of the inhabitants were selected indifferently from those they met in the street & without any trial whatsoever or previous suspicion of guilt, hung them because they would not make such discoveries as they were required to make.... Others were half strangled others beat & wounded & all filled with horror and consternation.....The soldiers pleasure is the only law"

Captain John Burganey was tragically killed in Newtownmountkennedy, County Wicklow on the 30th May 1798 at the age of 23.

Major Joseph Hardy, commander of Government troops in the County during the rebellion outlines the events leading up to John's death in a letter to Colonel Loftus.

Wicklow 30th May 1798
11 o'clock pm.
"Sir,

This morn at 2 o'clock a body of rebels from 500 to 1,000 taking advantage of the darkness of the morn, came down from their woods and rocks on Mount Kennedy, and having killed a Wicklow Yeoman express coming to me, forced into the town and set fire to the cavalry stables. The horses being removed that day to co-operate with me towards (illegible) no mischief was done but the burning of a few houses. The troops in the town consisted of the Ancient Britons, Mt. Kennedy Yeoman Cavalry and Antrim formed as fast as possible and before the rebels had possession of the market place, charged them with great impetuosity, in this onset I am sorry to relate Captain Burganey of the Ancient Britons was killed."......
"In Captain Burganey I have lost the aid of a most excellent Officer and a humane gentleman."

John was buried in the Church of Ireland cemetery in the small village of Newcastle, County Wicklow, 2 miles from where he was killed. There is a brief entry in the church records; "Burial in the parish of Newcastle, County Wicklow 1798, Captain John Burganey of the Ancient Britons buried June 1st."

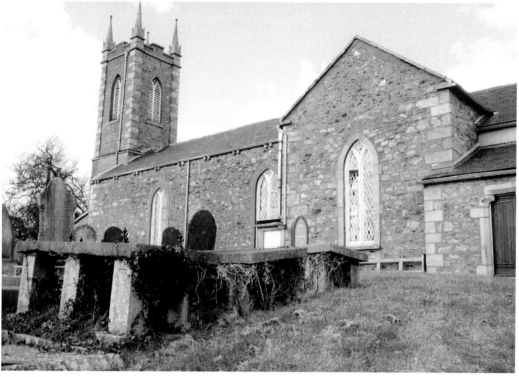

The Church of Ireland, Newcastle, Ireland

The following extract describing John Burganey's funeral, is from the manuscript of Luke Cullen who interviewed rebel participants and witnesses to the events of 1798. He is clearly not an impartial observer.

> *"Captain Burganey who fell the day before (Wednesday 30th May) in an attack on Newtown, was to be interred; Horse and foot attended in all the habiliments of mourning, to celebrate his funeral with all the pomp due to a fallen warrior. They marched with arms reversed, and stepped as slow as a surcharge of whiskey would permit. The Britons band struck up the Dead March in "Saul" while the fife and drum of the Yeomanry gave out some lively variations, such as "Boyne Water" and "Croppie Lie Down". Now and again there was*

a half choked utterance of blasphemy, plainly indicating that there was something concealed in the drunken silence.

It must be remembered that this land, so rich in the gifts of nature, with it's floral decorations, garlands and orange lilies, was promised to the young Britons before they left the Cambrian mountains. That promise had filled their ruthless souls with the "glories of the tented field."

When the last shovelful of clay fell on the mortal remains of Captain Burganey, and the troops had performed all the honours assigned for such an occasion in the military ritual for the gallant slain, Captain Archer gave the word-"fall in line, march- and "let slip the dogs of war..."

The interior of Newcastle church, Ireland where the funeral took place. The church was built in the 1780s on the site of a number of earlier churches

John was fortunate from the perspective that we found no evidence of a church service for any other Ancient Briton killed during the Rebellion. The remainder appear to lie in unmarked graves.

The following poem, copied from a manuscript appeared in the November 30th 1892 issue of 'Bye Gones' in the Oswestry and Border Counties Advertizer.

"Alas! And is the young Berganey gone
Youth, beauty, valour, all destroyed in one
For since his birth five lustres scarce had fled
When he was number'd with the silent dead
Tho' in his form appear'd each manly grace
Tho' beauty shone conspicuous in his face
Yet courage dwelt within his youthful heart
And in his breast each claimed a part
With gentle mercy justice was combin'd
And generous pity was with courage join'd
Bright truth and rigid honour too were there
With loyalty a virtue heavenly fair
True to his King his country and it's laws
He thought e'en life well lost in such a cause
Cover'd with wounds the youthful hero fell
And left the world the mournful truth to tell
Then mourn ye Britons mourn your Captain dead
The young, the brave, the good Berganey fled
But AH! What grief must strike a mothers heart
With such a son for ever doomed to part
A gentle sister too with tender breast
On his protection fondly hoped to rest
Yet he is gone alas! For ever fled
Both son and brother number'd with the dead
But 'twas not unaveng'd Berganey fell
His noble Britons have avenged him well
Yes my brave countrymen you have nobly fought
Nor once on loss of lives have thought
But freely ventured where your honour led
And gloried in the cause for which you bled
Nor shall ye be forgotten in the ground
The trump of fame shall spread your names around
And when upon Berganey's timeless bier
Soft pity sheds the gen'rous tear
And mourns with softest sighs his hapless lot
The Ancient Britons shall not be forgot
'Een victory's self shall for her Britons mourn
And twine her laurels round Berganey's urn."

Unfortunately for his family, John had not made a will. This must have caused many complications for his mother and sister in the running of the estate as there were court cases up to 35 years after his death concerning various long-term land leases.

It would appear that assistance was given to the family in estate matters by Bell Ince of Christleton. He may have been related. He moved to Pulford, and possibly took up residence at the hall.

Almost a quarter of a century after John's death, an initiative was taken, probably by the family, to replace his original tombstone. Major Joseph Hardy who had commanded Government troops in County Wicklow was honoured to supervise the work. He wrote the following letter to John's family addressed to Bell Ince;

Lamburton, Arklow
19th February 1821

"Sir,

I have agreed with the stone mason to erect a more handsome tomb according to plan and estimate which I have the honour to enclose for the approbation of the late Captain Burganey's sister and friends, as well as the smith's estimate amounting together to £30-9-7 and have given both earnest and the work is in progress as they did not like to begin the work for strangers in another country without £10 in hand and shall thank you to remit the amount as soon as convenient to W. George Sydney, 38, Cranault Street, London on my account.

I likewise send the inscription which if it does not please request to hear from you in a few posts as it may in this month be attended to your liking.

It will give me great pleasure to superintend the erecting of it and thus pay a tribute of respect to the memory of a mild unassuming gentleman and gallant brother soldier."

Enclosed with the letter was a copy of the proposed inscription which reads as follows:

"Underneath this stone are interred the remains of
John Burganey Esq. of Pulford
In the County of Cheshire
Late Captain in the regiment of Ancient British Cavalry
Aged 22 years
Who fell in action between the King's troops
And the rebels at Newtown Mnt. Kennedy
On the ? day of June 1798
Gloriously and Gallantly fighting for his King and Country"

John Burganey's tomb, Church of Ireland, Newcastle, County Wicklow, Ireland

Despite the fact that the horizontal stone is very badly weathered, it has been established, that the above text, with one exception, a correction in the date to 30th May is the actual inscription on the tomb. The stone does contain a slight error as they failed to notice that John was actually 23 when he was killed. This tragic end, marked the passing of the last in the male line of the Burganey's of Pulford.

John's mother, Ann, died in 1828 at the age of 81 and was buried in the local churchyard. Two years later Bell Ince aged 52 passed away. Finally, John's sister Ann, who had never married, died in 1847, aged 67. Pulford Hall and the estate were left to Bell's brother, Townsend Ince of Christleton.

Townsend Ince sold the Hall to the Duke of Westminster who leased it to the Massie family of Eccleston. In 1896 the Duke had the hall, which was reputed to be in poor condition, demolished. Three cottages were built in the park out of outbuildings which still survive today.

The site where Pulford Hall had once stood.
The area is still named the Park after the grounds which surrounded the hall.

References

With many thanks to Peter O'Donoghue, Blue Persuivant, College of Arms.

With kind permission of the Editor of the Oswestry and Border Counties Advertizer.

Captain John Burganey of the Ancient British Fencible Cavalry, Byrne and Chaloner, Hel Achau no. 101, June 2009.

The Ancient British Fencible Cavalry and the Irish Rebellion 1798, Byrne and Chaloner, forthcoming.

National Archives of Ireland ref. no. 620/17/30/25

National Archives of Ireland ref. no. 620/37/224

Insurgent Wicklow, Luke Cullen.

British Library, Harleian manuscripts, 2151 and 2153 (the manuscripts of Randle Holme III)

Cheshire Record Office, DWC/2 box 21 no. 3 (copy of page 2153 of the above manuscripts).

Flintshire Record Office D/DM/317/100

The History of the County Palatine and City of Chester, George Ormerod

Cheshire Record Office, QSF/20 f33

Cuckoo's Nest

By Kate Fairhurst and Audrey Gibson

The name Cuckoo's Nest might be expected to describe a peaceful, sleepy, rural retreat. In reality Cuckoo's Nest, on the northern edge of Pulford, is a hamlet which developed from Victorian times to provide a major source of local employment as the Eaton Estate works yard and brickworks. So how did it get its unusual name?

A map of the area drawn in 1776 shows the holder of the land to be Jane Ley, a widow from Lower Kinnerton, but no buildings nor place names are shown, although there is an arrow indicating the direction of 'The Oldfields'. The earliest reference we have found to the name Cuckoo's Nest is on a deed of sale dated 1826 when Robert, Earl Grosvenor purchased two cottages and their adjoining lands. These, which were called 'the Cuckoo's Nest', were bought for £300 from Daniel and Jane Ley of Great Boughton[1]. The cottages were on the west side of the turnpike road leading from Chester to Wrexham. At the time their occupants were Thomas Davies and Thomas Catherall, a general labourer who remained there with his family until the early 1850s.

These two cottages are still standing and are now known as Cuckoo's Nest Farm and Melling House. Cuckoo's Nest Farm still has its bread oven in the wall, a cheese room upstairs and an old copper boiler in the wash house. One of the old metal framed windows, shown overleaf, features interesting stained glass, but to date its origin and significance have not been explained. The owner is

The two cottages in 2007

currently restoring the cottage, and has found a George III penny dated 1797 under the quarry tiles in the oldest part of the building.

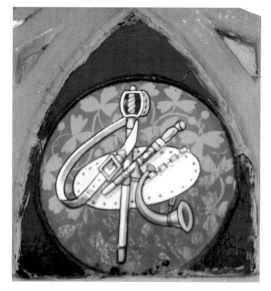

The stained glass in Cuckoo's Nest Farm

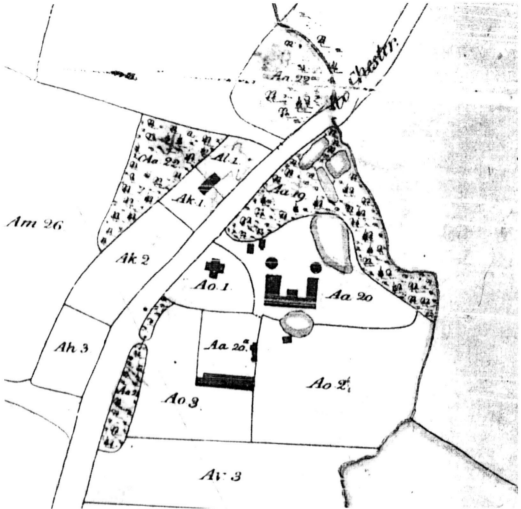

2 The Tithe Map of 1837

The section of the tithe map of 1837, illustrated, shows that some development has taken place in the area. The Cuckoo's Nest cottages can clearly be seen marked as Ak1 and Al1. Other buildings are shown on the opposite side of the Chester to Wrexham road from the cottages. The large, cross shaped house, Ao1, stood on the site of what is now called Clerk House. Its occupant at the time of the 1841 census was George Brough, a tile maker and farmer who came from Trentham in the Potteries. He and his wife Patience lived there with his niece Ann and four servants.* The area labelled Aa 20 on the tithe map was a tile yard and sheds, while that labelled Aa 20^a was a building yard and sheds. These were owned by the Marquess of Westminster, and were the beginnings of the estate yard.

The Eaton Estate continued to develop, and by the early 1860s two more pairs of cottages had been built on the Chester to Wrexham road near to the Cuckoo's Nest cottages and a further pair, attributed to the architect John Douglas, in the present lane to Oldfields (201 on the estate map). At that time the main route to Oldfields Farm was along a lane which ran from the Chester to Wrexham road, past 'The Elms' and then turned 90 degrees north to reach the farm. Oldfields lane was listed as an occupational road in the Eaton Estate Field Books[3].

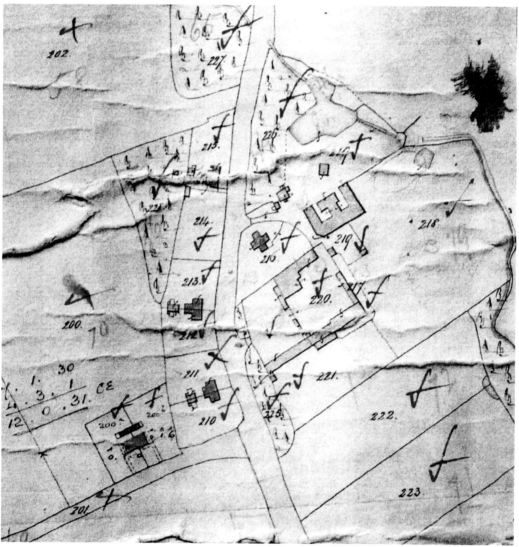

4 *The Eaton Estate map of 1865, Courtesy of the Grosvenor Family Archive.*

Some of the first occupants of the Cuckoo's Nest hamlet
taken from the 1861 census were:-

George Brough   - a master tile maker

Charles Powis   - a carpenter
                   (listed in 1871 as foreman of works)

John Grimley   - a house painter

William Salary   - a plumber/glazier

Thomas Roberts   - a wheelwright

George Charnock - a carpenter
                   (yard clerk in 1855)

Thomas Catherall - a labourer.

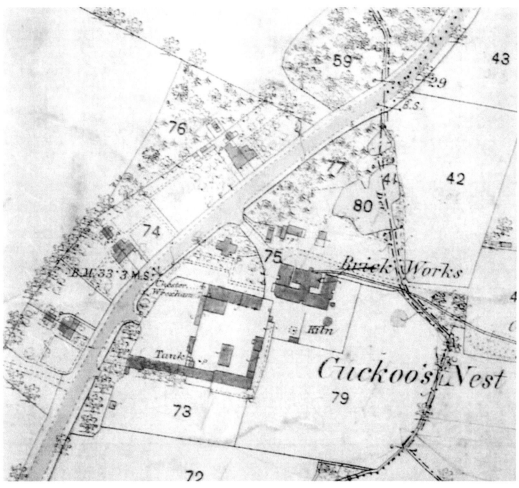

5 The Estate Map of 1875, Courtesy of the Grosvenor Family Archive.
Note that buildings are expanding and the name 'Cuckoo's Nest' is used.

The expansion of the Eaton Estate meant that there was a greater demand for building materials and labour and the yard took on a new importance. The estate yard was the place from which building work, maintenance and repairs to estate properties was administered and carried out. The Eaton Estate agent's quarterly accounts[6] at that time included bills for stationery, coal, slack and sundries for the works' yard horses. Horse-drawn transport was the primary means of carrying raw materials and other items. The 1863 accounts show that smiths' bellows, iron bars and a set of gearing were ordered from John E. Brassey. They also list payments for files and leather straps for the sawmill at Pulford yard and slack coal for the engine. The additional buildings shown on the 1866 estate map would have included an engine house, a sawmill, a smithy and stabling.

Following George Brough's death in 1870, Thomas Wynne, who lived in one of the Cuckoo's Nest cottages, became the brick and tile maker. Brough's wife, Patience, continued to live in the family home (Ao1). In the 1871 census she is listed as being a coal merchant. Living with her was her great nephew Henry Brough Jones (who was a carter), a servant and three lodgers. When she died in 1881 the house was demolished and rebuilt to a design by John Douglas as a new house for the clerk of works. It then became known as 'The Cuckoo's Nest' or 'The Nest'. The first clerk of works to live there was Joshua Smith.

Many employees were needed at the yard to maintain the estate buildings and workers' cottages. [7]Captain David Scotland, private secretary to the Duke, wrote a letter to his employer on 19th January 1883 concerning the hours of work and wages of the men at the Pulford yard. He noted that there were some forty men working at the yard, whose average weekly wage was twenty two shillings for a five and a half-day week. Although the wage was lower than that earned by similar workers in Chester, the deficiency was made up by cheap and comfortable housing and gardens. He also pointed out that wages in the north of England were as a rule higher than in the south. He felt that the attitude of the men who were employed in the yard was that they were 'there for life' and that this might induce some of them to be easy-going and waste time.

The dome-topped brick kilns with the newly built light railway, circa 1896. (Courtesy Plateway Press Collection)

By 1884 the accounts[8] show an increasing demand for bricks and pipes. The old brickworks was no longer adequate for this task. A new works was built further away from the estate yard (near to where the tall chimney now stands). This included a new shed with an iron roof, a new engine boiler and a new brick making machine. Thomas Wynne, the then foreman, was employed to level the ground and make concrete for new brick kilns. Two new circular dome top kilns were built; each had eight fires and could produce about twenty five thousand bricks in every firing. The site of the new brickworks can be seen on the Eaton Estate map of 1898 (see overleaf) and the big clay pits which served it are clearly visible. This map also marks the route of the newly built Eaton Light Railway.

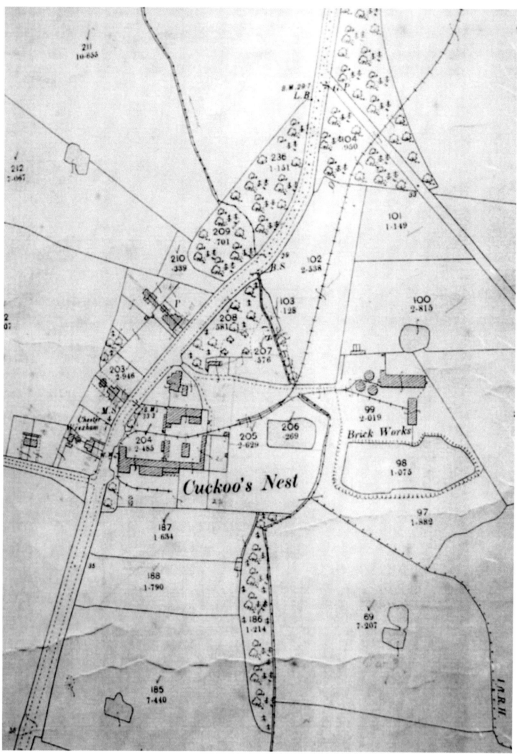

9The Eaton Estate map of 1898 Courtesy of the Grosvenor Family Archive

10 The Nest' – later 'Clerk House' (Courtesy of the Grosvenor Family Archive)

In 1919 portions of the Eaton Estate were sold, some privately and some at public auction. The sale of part of the western portion, which included Cuckoo's Nest, was reported in The Chester Chronicle of February 1st, 1919. The Chronicle stated that bidding was brisk at the auction held at the Grosvenor Hotel in Chester; eighty four lots being disposed of in as many minutes. Many of the 'model' cottages at Cuckoo's Nest were sold to the tenants

The Estate yard from Wrexham Road, (Courtesy of the Grosvenor Family Archive)

for around £320. One of the cottages at Cuckoo's Nest was sold to Oldfields farm. ** One was retained by the estate and later used as a lodging house for the apprentice foresters based at the woodyard, which was where the Grosvenor Garden Centre now stands. However the estate works, (comprising manager's house, offices, extensive workshops, yards, buildings, brick and tile works, pasture land and plantation), the whole extending to seventeen acres, was withdrawn at £4,500.

At some time between the sale and 1929 the brick and tile works was leased to the Atlas Stone Company, a firm which had other branches in the North and Midlands, and brick making continued. This firm was later to change its name to The Premier Stone Company because another business was using the name 'Atlas'. Mr Thomas Gibson, the managing director of Premier Stone recalls visiting Chester at this time as a boy of twelve and coming to his grandfather's brickworks at Cuckoo's Nest. At that time the estate yard was still being used by the Eaton Estate and the little train came through the yard but it no longer went to the brickworks. The clay was obtained manually from the ever- expanding clay pit close at hand. The bricks produced, which were of a pinkish colour and shot with yellow from the firing, were the type used for inside walls.

Local worker Wilf Stockton at the brickworks, June 1931

The Premier Stone Company had a long history at Cuckoo's Nest. During the Second World War the company was forbidden by the War Office to use its brick kilns because the glow from the fires presented a threat to national security as the enemy aircraft could easily identify the site. The company however did obtain a large contract from The Ministry of Works to produce pressed concrete frames for prefabricated huts which enabled it to remain in business.

After the war ended, the company did not receive any compensation for the loss of their brick-making business. The management decided to concentrate on pressed concrete, a business which continued for many years. One of the two tall chimneys was removed and huge silos for cement were installed. In the early 1960s rubble from the demolition of the old Eaton Hall and some from the old hospital was used to fill in a large portion of the clay pit.

It is only possible at present to estimate when the yard itself ceased to be used by the estate. The last clerk of works to live in the house known as 'The Nest' was James Morgan. He was a local man, promoted from being a carpenter and was there from 1922 until 1939 when he retired. After Morgan's departure, the site was let to R.Tyrer for his own business in 1939-1940 and then in 1941 to Evan Cheers, a local builder.

In 1945 John and Nancy Thompson leased the 'The Nest' and the estate yard. They had been established builders' merchants in Buckley. The business at Cuckoo's Nest was registered in Mrs Thompson's name and became well known in the area as 'Nancy Thompson's'. The main activity of the business

was the making and selling of breeze blocks, but other builders' supplies, such as sand, gravel, shale and bags of cement were also sold.

Thompsons had a fleet of twenty six lorries but not all of these were kept on site. These lorries not only delivered goods to customers but also collected raw materials. Ash was brought for the breeze blocks from the colliery at Llay. The best quality white ash came from Bowaters' paper works at Ellesmere Port. In the wintertime this was stored in the Bothy.

The breeze blocks were made in a hopper in the block yard, and then put in lines to dry. The lines of drying blocks can clearly be seen alongside the buildings to the left in the aerial photograph. The powdered cement used in making the breeze blocks was delivered in special bulk containers and piped into a silo close to the Wrexham road. On delivery days a fine layer of cement dust would fall over the local area, much to the annoyance of some of the residents.

Aerial view of the site in the 1960. (Courtesy of Aerial van Rhijn Photographer Brian Granger)

As many as one hundred and twenty workers were employed at the Cuckoo's Nest site in the 1960s. Many of them lived locally. These workers included office staff, machine operators, drivers, labourers, welders, mechanics and fitters. For six days workers 'clocked on' at the Clock

House at 7am and finished at 5.30pm. Some of those involved in the maintenance of the lorries and machines would also work on Sundays. Machines included bulldozers, diggers, forklift trucks and cranes.

The old buildings on the site were used for storing dry materials, engine parts and oil drums. Lorries were serviced under cover. Another building was converted into a canteen for the employees. Mrs Thompson's office was in the Clock House and from here, she could see all the comings and goings in the yard. Very little escaped her attention. In the single storey block which separated the two muddy courtyards were toilets for the men and a weighbridge office. The weighbridge which was alongside was also used by the police for checking vehicles. Open bays were constructed for storing sand and gravel, especially the white-grey gravel from the Minera lead mines which was sold for constructing drives. The council also stored its supply of salt for the roads and several fuel pumps were located on the site

Cleaning the weighbridge. (Courtesy of Mrs Margaret Evans)

The Thompsons ceased trading about 1992 and the site became an eyesore. Premier Stone ceased to trade, and two concrete firms, Pulford Precast and Dynamix took over. By 1994 suggestions were put forward to develop the whole site. This came to a head in 1996 when approval was received for an industrial estate to be built in place of the brickworks and for the Victorian buildings in the yard to be converted into offices. However, as a result of an appeal and the intervention of the then Secretary of State, the plans were overturned and had to be modified.

The Bell Meadow Business Park

The end result was as we see it today. The Bell Meadow Business Park, which is where the brickworks once stood, was completed in 2003. In ten purpose-built large buildings, at any one time it houses some twenty – thirty service sector businesses. It is a marked change from 'dirty' to 'clean' when compared with its previous existence. The only evidence of the site's past is the tall brickworks' chimney which remains as a feature and the clay pit which is now an ornamental pond.

Although Cuckoo's Nest can still be described as a hamlet, having neither shops nor a centre, it now comprises a total of twenty seven dwellings, its size almost doubling since the Second World War. The estate yard has been converted into eleven dwellings and the Bothy greatly extended into a large house.

Cuckoo's Nest was finally put on the map in 1996 when a sign was erected on Wrexham Road to show its existence.

*George Brough's gravestone can be seen in Pulford church yard. The inscription on this reads, 'This stone was erected by the Brethren of the Chester District of the Independent Order of Oddfellows, Manchester Unity of which the deceased was a Provincial Grand Master as a mark of their appreciation of his long and varied labours for the extension of Oddfellowship.' Could his labours for the extension of the Oddfellows movement be connected with The Earl Grosvenor Lodge which began in Pulford in 1840, around the time when Brough moved to Pulford?

**The tenant of this cottage had been killed in the First World War. None of his six children was old enough to take their father's place on the farm and consequently his widow and family were made homeless. This pre-dated the Welfare State, and the destitute family was taken in by the then Rector of Pulford who provided lodgings in return for domestic work.

References.

Courtesy of the Grosvenor Family Archive:
1.   ED.F10/1
3.   Eaton Estate Field Books EV.6674, 675.
4.   EM. 49
5.   EM. 74
6.   EV. 390, 391
7.   EP. 40/27
8.   EV. 401
9.   EM. 96
10. EM. 74

Courtesy of the Chester Record Office:
2. CRO EDT 336/1-2

Special thanks to Richard and Margaret Evans and Thomas Gibson for their personal memories and to Mia Jones.

A Social Perspective

By Marian Davies

The performance of Civic Duty is an important part of the life of any community. In this regard, Pulford has made its contribution to Cheshire and the City of Chester in recent times. Both the High Sheriff of Cheshire and the Mayor of Chester (Lord Mayor since 1992) have long histories going back several hundred years. The late Sir Donald Wilson of Oldfields Farm and Honorary Alderman Gerry Fair, recently of Brookside Farm, are two people in particular who deserve recognition for their past service to the wider community.

The High Sheriff of Cheshire

It was in 1985 that Mr Donald Wilson was appointed High Sheriff of Cheshire. Lady Wilson recalls "It was a busy and enjoyable year with many functions to attend and the arranging and hosting of a considerable number of events. The opportunity of meeting so many interesting people, including members of the Royal Family visiting Chester at this time, made Don's year of office both satisfying and memorable."

In the 1987 New Year's Honours Sir Donald Wilson received his Knighthood from the Queen.

Donald Wilson outside Oldfields Farm House in 1985 (Photo courtesy of Lady Wilson)

Mayor of Chester

After many years service as a local and city councillor, Cllr. Gerry Fair was appointed the 750th Mayor of the City of Chester in 1987.

The Mayor of Chester, Cllr. Gerry Fair & Mrs Margaret Fair
(Photo courtesy of the former Chester City Council)

Besides his civic duties Gerry ran the largest farm in the area at Brookside.   His service to the community was recognised when he was made an Honorary Freeman and Alderman of the City of Chester.

Rural District Council

In 1954 the Chester Rural District Council was formed and Edward Pritchard, who lived at The Elms, Pulford, represented the village on the council. On his retirement, Mrs Fidelia Fair took his place and became 'Chairman of the Council' in 1965. In 1973 the Rural District Council amalgamated with the Chester City Council and Mrs Fair became known as the 'City Councillor' representing Dodleston, Eccleston, Aldford and Poulton & Pulford. On her retirement in 1976 her son Gerry was voted on as 'Ward Councillor'.

Poulton and Pulford Parish Council

The Parish Council was formed in 1964 when the election of Parish Councillors took place on the 4th May that year. Over the years, the Parish Council has served the local community overseeing several important developments since the 1970s:

Church Bank
Construction of the Wrexham Bypass – A483
Fairmeadow
Pulford Court
Castle Hill
Burganey and Ivy Courts
Cuckoo's Nest
Brookside and the new farm at Poulton
Yew Tree
Mayfield

Pulford's Playing Field was acquired from the National Playing Field Association.

30 m.p.h. speed limit introduced in the village.

Local councillors visit the construction site of the new A483 Wrexham Bypass c.1986. (Photo courtesy of Melba Venables)

The Village Hall

For many years the Village Hall was the property of Eaton Estate and is understood to date back to the mid to late 1800s. It is thought that originally the building may have been cottages.

Before the First World War it was called the 'Reading Room' and was used strictly for men only. However, a letter dated 1924, discovered during research, shows that the newly formed Pulford Women's Institute was given permission to use the hall two evenings a month for their committee and monthly meetings.

The earliest minute books relating to the hall appear to be those of 1930, when quite a lot of work was carried out on the building and a new tenancy agreement was drawn up with the Eaton Estate. From then on the impression is given that it was used for many activities in the village.

A letter was circulated around the village in 1968 when it was proposed to make changes to the hall and we are able to relate what happened. A further agreement was drawn up with Eaton Estate for twenty-five years at a preferential rent and in c.1970 three Trustees were appointed. All repairs and alterations were then to be undertaken by a Management Committee with the various organisations using the hall being represented. The late Tom Dodd should be recognised for the considerable amount of work he did to help maintain the hall. The hall was then improved with a new kitchen, toilets and main hall extension. Local volunteers carried out most of this work. The floor of the main hall was replaced by one removed from the 'Majestic Ballroom' in Chester, which was closed and the building put to an alternative use.

The team of volunteers working on the extension to the hall in May 1970.
From left: Tom Dodd, Gerald Mallinson, Jim Dryland, Francis Glew,
Roger Vincent, Robert Bradshaw & Richard Fair.
(Photo courtesy of Roger Vincent)

Later (c.1976) the Committee Room was added and this was paid for with a 'Bond' scheme supported by local people. Subsequently, activities were held to raise money and the bonds were repaid over a period of several years. The Eaton Estate lease was then further extended.

In 1998 the car park was extended and the entrance was moved from the front to the side (land given by Bell Meadow Development). At this time, the Duke of Westminster decided to present the Village Hall to the Poulton and Pulford Parish Council.

The Duke of Westminster being greeted by Roger Vincent, Parish Clerk, Marian Davies, Chairman of the Parish Council and Mrs Margaret Fair, Chairman of the Village Hall Committee at the Handover Ceremony.
(Photograph published courtesy of the Chester Chronicle)

The bus shelter, which stood on the edge of the original car park, was given to the village in 1944 by Mr. & Mrs. Moore of Iron House, Dodleston Lane, to commemorate their 50th Wedding Anniversary. During the Bell Meadow Development programme the shelter was moved to its present position.

THIS SHELTER WAS PRESENTED TO THE PARISH OF PULFORD AND POULTON BY Mʀ & Mʀˢ J.T. MOORE. TO COMMEMORATE THEIR GOLDEN WEDDING 1894 MARCH 28ᵀᴴ 1944.

During the years from 1930 to the present day many organisations have used the hall, these include Pulford Women's Institute from 1924; Pulford Youth Club that had many activities including dancing and weekly meetings from the late 1940s to mid 1950; weekly Whist Club in 1960 and 1970; Pulford Players – a very successful amateur dramatic group; Guides and Brownies, but they could not continue due to lack of children. The Hall remains a venue today with the Bridge Club, Ex YMCA members Table Tennis Group, Pulford Painters art group, Pulford & Poulton Local History Group and Pulford Handbell Ringers. It is also a popular venue for private parties at weekends. We are very proud of our Village Hall which is looked after by a very dedicated group of local parishioners.

Societies and Organisations

Pulford W.I.

Formed in 1924, Pulford W.I. has maintained a good membership over the years, taking an active part in most Cheshire Federation W.I. events; especially at the Cheshire County Show – exhibiting and gaining awards. During the Second World War, Pulford took part in the 'canning & pie scheme' to help support the food supply. Evidence of their handicraft work can be seen in the Pulford Church kneelers, W.I table cloths and the Parish collage in the village hall. More recent activities have included walking, drama, darts and quizzes.

The W.I. Collage of the Parish

Pulford WI c.1930 in Iron House garden

WI members celebrating Marian Davies'(centre) Cheshire Rural Women's Award in 2005, with from the left Melba Venables, Janet Linn, Jenny Nethercott, Margaret Fair, Margaret Glew & Madge Dodd.

Pulford & Poulton Local History Group

An evening guided tour of the gardens at Erddig by the Head Gardner, Mr Glyn Smith. 15th September 2004.

During the History Group's ten years of existence it has maintained a monthly schedule of talks from guest speakers on a host of local history topics. Visits to local places of interest also feature in the group's programme. The group also manages an archive of local historical documents and photographs that have been donated mainly by local people.

A day visit to the Rüg Estate, the home of Lady Newborough, near Corwen, 27th April 2006.

The History Group hosted a Civic Trust 'History & Heritage Weekend' on the life of the village in September 2002.

Here, Mrs Margaret Fair, Chairman of the History Group, welcomes the Sheriff of Chester, Cllr Edward Walley and his lady to the Open Weekend

Pulford Painters

Originally under the direction of 'Cheshire Life' Artist, Gordon Wilkinson, many of the group started painting together years ago and came to Pulford in 2003. The group meets every week in the Village Hall and in recent years has held a popular annual exhibition of members' work. The group holds workshops with invited experts who cover a wide range of subjects to suit all needs and abilities.

The Art Exhibition in 2009. (Photo courtesy of Dr. Robin Glaze)

The Village Hall has been the centre of village life for many decades and continues to serve the local community, attracting many organisations with its excellent facilities and warm appeal.

Acknowledgements.

Thanks are expressed to Roger Vincent for his help with this chapter.

Around the Village

By Michael Nethercott

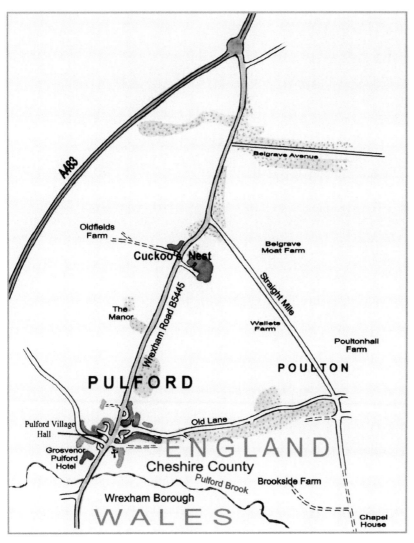

The three designated centres of Cuckoo's Nest, Pulford and Poulton lie approximately one mile apart in triangular formation and are connected by three roads: Straight Mile between Cuckoo's Nest and Poulton; Wrexham Road joining Cuckoo's Nest and Pulford; and Old Lane linking Pulford with Poulton.

Pulford (including Cuckoo's Nest) and Poulton occupy a rural setting in the south-west corner of Cheshire on the border with north-east Wales, some five miles to the south-west of Chester, an International Heritage City. The local boundary between England and Wales is denoted by the Pulford Brook. Pulford is approximately 15 metres above sea level and is protected from the south-west by the Clwydian Hills, which results in a lower than average rainfall locally than that of the region generally.

The character of Pulford and Poulton has been well preserved through the twentieth century. In earlier times, the influence of the Grosvenor family was paramount, especially during the nineteenth century with the growth in farming and the building of tenant farms, farmhouses and farm workers' cottages. Many of these buildings survive to the present day as will be seen in the John Douglas chapter, even though conversion of some farm buildings into superior dwellings has occurred in recent years.

OLD LANE

With the emphasis on farming in the past and the designation of green belt areas, housing development has been constrained, with the result that the most recent development has taken place on brown field sites and by the conversion of existing farm buildings.

Old Lane, as its name suggests, has a long history and in maps dating back to the 1790s is shown to proceed from Poulton to Eaton, then to Handbridge and over the Old Dee Bridge to Chester City.   Similarly, Wrexham Road, known in the late 1700s as the 'Great Road from Chester' joined with the Poulton road in Handbridge and thence into the city.   Now, Old Lane terminates at the junction with Straight Mile, although the continuation of the old road entering the Eaton Estate is still in evidence.

Old Lane accommodates a variety of architectural styles towards the centre of the village with the few dwellings having been built from the 1920s through to 2008.

In early spring, Old Lane displays a mass of snow-drops over quite a distance, making it a real 'Snowdrop Walk', followed a little later by daffodils, all planted by Honorary Alderman Gerry Fair of Brookside Farm in the 80s for the enjoyment of the people of the parish.

At the junction of Old Lane with Straight Mile, the old building of Poulton School, now a private residence, can be seen on the left.

Straight Mile

The entrance to the old Poulton to Eaton & Eccleston road, now closed,
at the junction with Straight Mile

The Green, Poulton

In the first half of the nineteenth century, the then Marquess of Westminster had a new drive constructed, called 'Pulford Approach', to provide direct access from Eaton Park to the Wrexham Road at Church Bank, Pulford, passing through a wooded area between Poulton and Pulford. A map of 1820 clearly shows 'Approach road to Eaton' coincident with what became known as Pulford Approach, corresponding to the time of the First Marquess of Westminster. The North and South Lodges at the entrance to Pulford Approach, now closed, are now private residences.

North Lodge (left) and South Lodge as seen from Church Bank

The Spinney in the middle of Pulford provides a pleasant boundary to Castle Close, built c.1963

Opposite Castle Close is the small but neat cul-de-sac of 'Fairmeadow' (mid 1980s) occupying land that once belonged to the Fairs' of Brookside Farm.

Opposite Church Bank is Dodleston Lane, another of the old routes going back to the eighteenth century leading to Dodleston, Kinnerton and Hawarden.

Dodleston Lane

Castle Hill below (mid 1990s) takes its name from the site, opposite, of Pulford Castle, a medieval motte & bailey.

The largest of the residential developments in Pulford occurred in the late 1990s on the site of the old Chaloner's Yard. Thirty five properties, including cottage and barn conversions were built in Burganey Court and Ivy Court to the exacting standards of Bell Meadow. Reclaimed 'Cheshire Brick' was used in the construction of many of them, and some features originating from the nineteenth century John Douglas designs were recreated, notably decorative gable ends, string coursing at first floor level and diamond 'cross hatching' in the brickwork. This development contributed significantly to the local population at a time when, ironically, Pulford's only shop was about to close.

Wrexham Road, Pulford, looking north from the junction with Old Lane, with the Pump Cottages seen behind 'D.M. Performance Cars' Garage

Pulford Railway Station

Not very likely you may say! However, Pulford Railway Station existed in the middle of the nineteenth century. Bradshaw's first railway timetable to include 'Pulford & Dodleston' Station was issued for March 1847 – the line opened in November 1846.

The station, subsequently called 'Pulford Station', was located approximately half a mile to the west of Pulford Church, close to the present level crossing. It comprised two platforms for the double track existing at that time and was served by trains between Chester and Shrewsbury on the Great Western Railway from Paddington to Birkenhead. William Wildig, as will be seen in the list of occupations for 1851 in Village Enterprise, was the station master. With the neighbouring station of Rossett close by Pulford Station was closed to passengers early in 1855, but Pulford Sidings remained in use for goods traffic until 1959. The line was reduced to a single track in 1986.

Bradshaw's timetable of January 1854 (courtesy of John Dixon)

From Bradshaw's Railway Timetable of January 1854, below, it will be seen that there were three classes of travel in those days with the fares from Chester to Pulford of one shilling for 1st class, 9d for 2nd class and 5½d 3rd class.

☞ **Further alterations expected about the 3rd instant.**

CHESTER, WREXHAM, RUABON, OSWESTRY, and SHREWSBURY.—Shrewsbury and Chester.

Engineer, Alexander Mackintosh. Secretary, John Nicholls.

[Railway timetable — Up and Down trains between Chester, Wrexham, Ruabon, Oswestry, Shrewsbury, with fares in 1st, 2nd and 3rd class, for Week Days and Sundays. Stations listed include Victoria Sta., Manchester, Liverpool, Chester, Saltney, Pulford, Rossett, Gresford, Wrexham, Rhos, Ruabon, Llangollen Rd, Cefn, Chirk, Presgwyn, Gobowen Junc., Oswestry, Whittington, Rednal, Baschurch, Leaton, Shrewsbury.]

BIRMINGHAM, WOLVERHAMPTON, and SHREWSBURY.—Shrewsbury and Birmingham.

The Ellesmere Canal

A Canal by Pulford?

Maps dating back to the late 1700s show there were serious intentions to construct a canal passing close to Pulford, known at the time as the 'Ellesmere Canal Navigation'. This was to connect the rivers Mersey near Ellesmere Port, with the Dee at Chester and the Severn near Shrewsbury.

A formal proposal for the Ellesmere Canal was launched in 1791 and an Act of Parliament passed in 1793. Thomas Telford was appointed General Agent to oversee the programme. Several plans for the canal were produced. One published in 1795 shows the route passing through Rough Hill and Cuckoo's Nest, skirting Pulford to the east and continuing on through Wrexham to Ruabon en route to Shrewsbury. The route also passed close to many extensive and valuable collieries; lime stone, slate and other quarries; iron works and lead mines. This would have opened a safe and easy transportation for the carriage of goods and merchandise by water between Liverpool and Shrewsbury. The distance from the Severn to the Dee was shown as 47 miles and from the Dee to the Mersey as 8 miles 3 furlongs.

The relatively easy section of the canal from Ellesmere Port to Chester was built and in use by 1795. The Llangollen section was started some two years later. However, by 1805 the section from the Dee at Chester to Ruabon had been abandoned as uneconomic. Doubtless the difficult terrain would have been a factor.

How the character of Pulford and Poulton might have changed had the canal, running close by with all its commercial traffic of the nineteenth century and recreational traffic of today, come into existence. However, this was not to be – and may be for the better?

The Ellesmere Canal

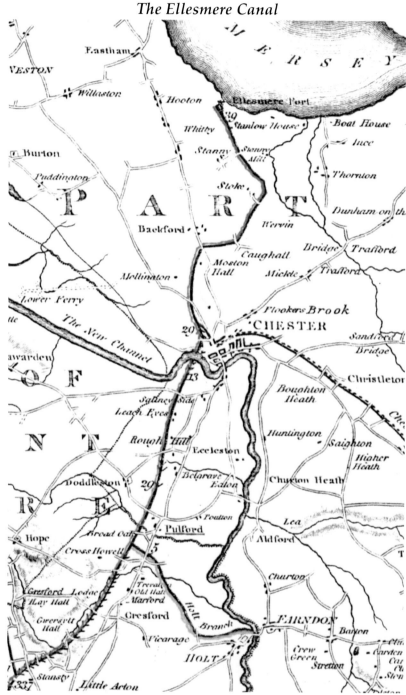

*The plan of 1796 above shows an alternative route for the canal
passing to the west of Pulford and continuing up the Gresford rise,
through what would probably have been a staircase of locks.
Note also, the Holt Branch of the canal passing to the south of Pulford
to Farndon. (Plan courtesy of Peter Moore Dutton)*

This final chapter, like all the others throughout this book, provides an aspect of our history 'through the ages'. There has been a wealth of history to record – and still more to do. That history has shaped our present day environment in which we now live. Our history is our heritage, for good or ill. I believe we in Pulford and Poulton have a heritage of which we can be proud.

One objective of our History Group's Constitution is 'to carry out research into our local history and communicate discoveries to a wider audience'. I suggest the Book Team has succeeded in doing just that.

Acknowledgements.

Terry Broadhurst
Canal Maps Archive website
Wikipedia: Ellesmere Canal

Acknowledgements

In addition to the acknowledgements in the individual chapters, the Book Team wish to thank especially the following for their kind help and support in the preparation of this book:

His Grace the Duke of Westminster and the Trustees of the 4th Duke of Westminster's Settlement for access to the Grosvenor Family Archive.

The Queen's Gallery and Miss Katie Hollyoaks.

Cheshire Community Action for their 'Grass Roots' Grant.

Jonathan Pepler, County Archivist & Staff at the Cheshire Record Office.

The Chester Grosvenor Museum.

The Chester History & Heritage.

The Chester Military Museum.

The RAF Museum, Cosford.

Dominic Byrne, for his contribution to the Burganey chapter.

John Hess, for general help and advice on printing and publication.

Martin Hughes, for computer work and photography.

Harold J. Storey, Chairman, Cheshire Heraldry Society.

Paul Williams.

Reference:
Inside front cover – Map O.S. 1875 1st Edition
C.R.O. Ref. XLVI 6.

grassroots
grants

Managed by the Community Development Foundation

The Book Team

Cllr. Keith Board

Gaenor Chaloner

Marian Davies

Mike Emery

Margaret Fair (Chairman, History Group)

Kate Fairhurst

Audrey Gibson

Margaret Hughes

Jennifer Nethercott

Michael Nethercott (Team Leader)

Derek Venables

Tom Walker

Index

Taken from the text & illustrations, but not from the acknowledgements.

Persons mentioned

Photo – Martin Hughes